What
Was He
Thinking?

Other Books by Mike Bechtle

What
Was He
Thinking?

The Woman's Guide
to a Man's Mind

Dr. Mike Bechtle

SPIRE

© 2016 by Mike Bechtle

Published by Revell
a division of Baker Publishing Group
PO Box 6287, Grand Rapids, MI 49516-6287
www.revellbooks.com

Spire edition published 2021
ISBN 978-0-8007-3953-9

Previously published in 2016 as *I Wish He Had Come with Instructions*

Printed in the United States of America

Published in association with the literary agency of Alive Communications, Inc., 7680 Goddard Street, Suite 200, Colorado Springs, CO 80920, www.alivecommunications.com.

21 22 23 24 25 26 27   7 6 5 4 3 2 1

To Lucy
I prayed that my son would find a wife
who would bring him joy.
You far exceeded my expectations and brought us
unexpected joy as well. What an amazing gift you are to us!

Para Lucy
Yo oraba que mi hijo puede encontrar una esposa
para traerle alegría.
Tu has excedido mis expectativas bastante y trajiste alegría
a nosotros también. ¡Que regalo asombroso tu eres
para nosotros!

Contents

Introduction

Talking into Thin Air

You're driving somewhere with your man. It's about dinnertime and you've had a long, exhausting day. You're thinking it would be nice to stop somewhere for dinner instead of having to go home and find the energy to prepare something (even if he helps).

So you say, "Would you like to stop for dinner someplace?"

He replies, "Not really."

Based on the differences between how men and women tend to process information, you might be hurt by his response. *Doesn't he care about how tough my day was? Why is he being so inconsiderate? Why does he get to decide what we do?*

It's possible that your interpretation is accurate. Maybe he doesn't care and he is inconsiderate. But more likely he didn't realize what was behind your words. He heard a question asking his input, so he shared an honest response. Maybe he's equally exhausted and wants to retreat to the safety of home instead of fighting a crowded restaurant. Or maybe he's a little concerned about finances and feels like it would be better to save money.

You feel like he should understand what you need and want. He feels like he answered your question so there is no need to explain things. Same words, different interpretation. The rest of the evening can become tense because of unspoken expectations and emotions.

It's a language barrier—two people using the same words but not connecting. If we assume that the other person shares our exact meaning and understanding, we're setting ourselves up for frustration.

Age or position doesn't matter:

Teenage girls begin dating without any understanding of how guys think. All they know is what they observe from experience. So they think they understand and wonder why it's so challenging.

A new manager comes in and his actions seem to contradict what he says. But you can't challenge the boss, right? So all you can do is try to figure him out.

Newlyweds learn quickly that their new spouse doesn't fit the image they expected and wonder what happened after the ceremony ended.

Moms wonder why their sons are so radically different from their daughters and how to make sense of their perspective—especially during their teen years.

When you want to develop a new skill, you take courses, read books, or attend seminars to learn new perspectives.

If you want to improve your communication skills with men, it's worth the investment of time and energy to make it happen.

It's time to begin that journey.

Everybody's Different

I'm a morning person. I generally wake up before sunrise, and I'm fully awake within about five minutes. Give me a cup of coffee to start my day, and I'm at my freshest. I'm mentally at my best. By 9:00 at night I have trouble forming multisyllable words or walking upright. When my head hits the pillow, I'm usually asleep in seconds.

My wife, Diane, tends to be a night person. Her job often gets her up early by necessity, so she's learned to function in the morning. But she naturally operates best later in the day or early evening. It often takes her a lot longer to go to sleep because her mind hasn't settled down yet.

We discovered the problem about two weeks into our marriage. We had settled into bed for the evening, and I was dropping off to sleep when I heard the four words that men dread: "We need to talk."

For her, it was a logical time. She had been thinking about an issue all day long. As a young husband I panicked because I didn't want her to think I didn't care. So I told myself, *Don't fall asleep . . . don't fall asleep . . .* while she described the situation. She assumed that her new, caring husband would be happy to talk through the issue. I really was interested, and I really did care. She kept talking, and I kept dropping off.

She was talking into thin air.

We had to do some damage control after that. But because of it, we realized that we're different. Part of it is the morning/night person scenario, but it's more than that. There are real differences between us, just because she's a woman and I'm a man.

Those differences can cause some challenges in communication when we don't understand them.

The Reality of Differences

"I don't get it," a friend told me. "I just don't understand men."

"What's going on?" I asked.

"When we were dating," she continued, "I was the most important thing in his life. He pursued me. He brought me flowers. He would call me for no reason. He left notes on my windshield while I was at work. He surprised me constantly, and he won my heart. So I married him."

"Then what happened?"

"I found out where he got the flowers," she said. "He would stop by the local cemetery and take them off of graves."

"And that bothered you?"

"Of course!" she responded. "He acted like it was a wise, practical choice because the flowers had done their job, and they would just go to waste and get thrown away. I told him it was disgusting, but he just didn't get it. He's such a good man, and this seems so out of character. What was he thinking?"

That's the big question: *What is a man thinking?*

The answer isn't a simple one. The only thing we can say for sure is that what a man is thinking is different from what a woman is thinking. We can debate the topic all day, but we know from experience that men and women aren't the same.

In the past few years, there has been a lot of emphasis on equality in the workplace. Women have never had the same opportunities as men, and legislation has opened those doors—and rightfully so.

But the transition has been challenging. The message came across as "men and women are the same." It sounded good to minimize differences so everyone would be treated equally. Men and women would dress professionally and sit around a conference table and commit to treating each other with respect. The doors were open, and opportunity was available to everyone.

But then they started talking to each other. And the collective response was . . . "Huh?"

With the best of intentions, people try to make equality work. They want to treat working relationships, marriages, dating, and friendships with the respect they deserve. People care about each other and want to build the best into the lives of others.

But "equality" is different from "equal." There *are* differences between men and women. The place it shows up most clearly is in how we communicate. Women can't figure out men, and men can't figure out women. The solution is not "fixing" those differences but rather understanding them.

We can legislate behavior. But trying to change the innate differences between men and women is like voting on which direction the sun moves across the sky. We can cast our vote, but we'll still be frustrated if we picked the wrong direction.

There are plenty of books that debate gender roles and societal issues. This isn't one of them. It's simply a guide for women to understand, from a man, what goes on inside the male mind. The more a woman knows about what's really happening in there, the easier it will be to use that knowledge to connect effectively with the men in her life.

I've talked to women who were frustrated because their attempts to connect were like trying to change a tire while their car was moving at sixty-five miles per hour. It wasn't working. One friend said, "I thought it would be easy, because we have so much in common. But when we start talking, I feel like we're speaking different languages. I wish he had come with instructions."

There's another issue here: every man is different, just as every woman is different. If we use a stereotype that says "all men are this way" and "all women are this way," we'll be in big trouble. I've read those kinds of books, and thought, *Yeah, but that doesn't sound like me.* So there's an important filter we need to apply as we begin this journey: *everyone is unique.*

There are some relevant generalities, but that's where we'll begin—recognizing that everyone is different. The ideas we talk about will be a starting point for discussion. In fact, you'll probably find some good conversation starters from the things you discover. It's a tool for exploration, not for slapping labels on the guys in your life.

Yes, it would be great if men came with instructions—but we don't. Neither do women, or kids, or bosses, or neighbors, or in-laws. There are some generalities that apply to relationships with these people, but they only provide a starting place. We have to figure people out one by one.

Who Stole the Instructions?

One of my favorite photos is from when my first grand-daughter, Averie, came home from the hospital. My daughter is holding her in the sink for her first bath, and my son-in-law is holding an instruction sheet from the hospital, trying to figure out how to do it. The bewildered look in their eyes seems to say, "So, what do we do with this kid?"

In the twelve years since that event, they've figured it out step-by-step, and Averie is turning out great. But I'm sure they've often wished they had instruction sheets for different stages of the journey.

Figuring out how to communicate with men is kind of like driving a car. Every car has brakes, a gas pedal, a steering wheel, headlights, and a place to put gas in. But sometimes things are in different places. I recently rented a car and couldn't find the button to open the fuel door. Fortunately, the instruction manual was in the glove compartment, and I was able to look it up. (The button was in a totally random place and I never would have found it.)

If I follow the instructions for a car, I get predictable results. That doesn't apply when it comes to people, because everyone is different. There are a lot of things that are consistent about men, but we can't follow "one-size-fits-all" instructions and expect unfailing results. We can learn the basic skills of communication and relationships, but the process is dynamic and fluid.

This is not an instruction manual; it's an *understanding* manual. You won't get a list of absolutes or a process to follow that guarantees perfect communication with men. Instead, you'll get a clear sense of what goes on in a man's mind and how it's different from what goes on in a woman's mind. You'll understand why men think the way they do, even if those differences don't make complete sense to you.

My wife, Diane, pointed out that there are a lot of books written by men telling women what they should do. Even if the advice is sound, it's written from a male perspective. It's like a fish giving swimming lessons to a bird.

I agree, so I'm going to be cautious. My male mind can't grasp how the female mind works. But I've studied those differences and learned how to appreciate and respect them and work with them. My goal isn't to give canned answers, though I'll share my ideas and observations. My primary objective is to walk with you as an interpreter or guide as you explore the landscape of the male mind.

I was leading a seminar once for the largest electric utility in California, and the director of safety was in the class. I asked him what his job consisted of. He said, "My job is to keep people from dying." As I pressed further, he continued, "Electricity can kill people if you don't respect it. So I make sure that people know what can happen and then make the right choices when they're working with it. A couple of people die every year because they take it for granted."

"Honestly," he continued, "I don't understand electricity. I have my degree in it, but I still have trouble grasping the concept of how it works. But I have the utmost respect for it, and I've learned how to work with it to get the best results. Our people don't have to understand it completely, but they have to know how it works so they keep from getting hurt while capturing its power."

I thought that was a great illustration. Women will never fully understand exactly how a man's mind works because it's outside of their frame of reference. But if they recognize what's happening, they can use that level of respect to keep the relationship safe.

Understanding Men—A No-Brainer

A man's brain is his control center. Everything he does and thinks comes from his brain. So if you want to know how to communicate with a man, you need to know what's going on inside his brain. If you get the brain right, it explains everything else.

I can't tell you what a specific man is thinking, but we can go on a tour of his brain. I'll be your guide. We'll stop at a number of "scenic lookout points," and I'll highlight the landmarks. I'll point out the traps and danger zones, and where you might encounter quicksand and toxic waste. We'll also climb the peaks to see the incredible view that you might miss if you're stuck in the swamp.

When we're finished, you'll have a sense of what's going on in a man's mind. It will be different for each guy, but you'll know what to look for. The trail will begin to feel more accessible. With a clearer perspective of the territory, you'll be able to customize your communication so it becomes an effective way of building connection.

Communication—The Key to Connection

Women can't just read a book about how men think and expect things to be different. That's a starting place, but understanding needs to be put into practice through communication. If we can get our communication right, our relationships have a great chance of improving. If we don't get our communication right, it'll be hard to improve our relationships.

When men and women talk, they're engaging in cross-cultural communication. Even though they might speak the same language, the words carry different meaning. He says, "I'm hungry." She could think, *He's expecting me to fix him something*. That might be true, but he could have been just stating a fact with no expectations. If either person makes assumptions about what the other person means, it can lead to tough conversations.

That's true in any type of relationship, whether marriage, family, employment, or friendship. Women are going to encounter men in every part of their lives. Women need to see men accurately, not as someone who needs to be repaired so he thinks the way she does. It's not about change; it's about connection.

How This Book Is Different

When I started my research, I studied what had already been written on this subject. I found resources on building relationships, strengthening marriages, and overcoming the sticking points that happen between people. A few of those books were written specifically about how to understand men. Most of them fit into one or more of these categories:

- They were written by women, based on their own experience with men.

- They were about male/female relationships rather than focusing just on the uniqueness of men.
- They were filled with advice, suggesting courses of action to take.
- They were based on opinion rather than research.
- They were research-based and felt like a psychological treatise.

Most of them offered great perspectives and added value for the reader. They met a specific need. The one thing I didn't find was a simple, commonsense approach to understanding how a man thinks.

This book is a man's attempt to "let you in." I want to show you around the territory of a man's mind. If you can learn the basics of how men operate, you'll have a foundation for communicating effectively with the men in your life. Discovering a man's uniqueness and perspective can take the mystery out of that communication.

When I told women I was writing this book, they usually shared a sense of relief: "That's exactly what I've been looking for." When I told men I was writing it, there was an overwhelming sense of dread: "No! Don't give away our secrets!"

This book isn't designed to give either side an advantage. It's a road map for conversational and relational success. It's drawn from the research of others, as well as my own background. Not only have I lived in the male brain for a long, long time but I've also spent my career studying people in a variety of settings. I've been a college professor, a minister, a mentor, and a coach, and have taught over three thousand seminars as a corporate consultant. My doctorate is in higher and adult education, which is where I first learned the basics of how people think.

I don't know everything there is to know about every man's brain. My experience just means that I've had a bunch of opportunities to watch human behavior and interact with people, and I want to share those observations with you. I'm not asking you to agree with everything I say. My goal is to provide a glimpse into the mind of men so you can strengthen your relationships with them.

We'll cover topics such as:

- What to look for during both high-stress and low-stress situations
- Why he won't talk or let you in
- How men listen, and how it's different from how women listen
- What he means by what he says
- The illusion of communication
- What's behind his choices
- What a grown-up relationship looks like
- How his past has shaped his present
- What drives a man
- What he needs that only a woman can provide
- Why he can't see dirt
- What his emotions look like
- How he cares

That's where we're headed. It's a journey of understanding, and I'm eager to show you around. You probably picked up this book to understand your husband or boyfriend better, so that's where we'll focus. But you'll be able to apply what you learn here to male bosses, friends, or relatives too.

So, let's get started. We're at the trailhead, and we're ready for an adventure together.

Enjoy the journey!

WAIT—You Need to Sign a Waiver for the Trip

Before we move on, there's an important disclaimer: *this book is written with healthy males in mind.*

Not all men are healthy. Some are controlling and selfish, and they have issues that are deeply embedded from early life experiences, trauma, or dysfunction.

Every man has moments where he acts irresponsible and self-centered. It's not unique to men; we all do it. That's usually where tough conversations surface, and this book will provide the tools and techniques needed to deal with those times.

When those toxic behaviors become the primary way a man operates, it's a pattern that goes beyond the scope of this book. While taking this journey, you might find that the toxic sites in your man's brain have flooded the landscape. If that's the case, self-help books become ineffective. It's time for a professional approach.

If I have a headache, I'll take an aspirin. But if I have a heart attack, I need the expertise of a trained cardiologist. If I try to treat it myself, it could be fatal. This book is a guide for understanding a good, healthy man who is human and imperfect. That's the scope of our mission and the foundation for our discussion.

PART 1

The Care and Feeding of a Man

My granddaughter got a box of worms in the mail today. I was at their house helping my daughter, Sara, with a few projects for the morning. Her kids were at a summer session at church, so Sara and I worked together until it was time to pick them up. She went to get them, and I stayed in the garage with the door open.

The FedEx truck pulled up, and the driver got out and handed me a small package. I took it in the house and went back to work.

When Averie came home, she was excited to see the box. She pulled the tab to open it, took out the packing material, pulled out a small round box, and opened that. She was thrilled to show me the contents: dozens of short, wiggly worms.

Averie has a pet bearded dragon, a cool-looking reptile named Leia (after Princess Leia of *Star Wars* fame). She saved her money to purchase her and keeps her in a terrarium up in her room. It has a shelter for Leia to sleep in, a food bowl, rocks to climb on, and a heating lamp to sun herself on the rocks.

It also has a hammock.

Leia is one happy bearded dragon. Why? Because she's well taken care of. Averie spent a lot of time studying bearded dragons before she bought one. She studied what they eat, how they sleep, and what kinds of conditions are ideal. She cleans out her terrarium on a regular basis, and even takes Leia for walks in the backyard on a leash.

I'd be happy too!

Even adults put lots of energy into studying our pets to find out everything we can about them. With that knowledge, we don't complain that they don't talk or play team sports with us. We discover what they're like and what they need to thrive, and we do everything to make sure their needs are met. We have realistic expectations. When that happens, we find a lot of joy in having them around.

That's true with men as well. Women have specific, unique needs, and men have different needs. If those needs are met, they're free to grow into the men they were designed to be. If those needs aren't met, they'll spend all their time in the hammock.

As we begin this book, let's hear what those needs are, directly from the source. We'll look at what's going on inside a man's head, both from current research and from his own perspective. Studying men and learning as much as possible about them will give women the best chance for developing fulfilling relationships in the future.

1

Men Are from Earth, Women Are from Earth

Over the years, we've bought a lot of do-it-yourself furniture. It's become a familiar process:

- Open the box
- Look for the instructions (or at least my wife looks for them)
- Lay out all the pieces
- Try to follow the instructions
- Get frustrated
- Eat cookies

The instructions read as though they were written by someone who had never seen the actual pieces. Their "step-by-step" process becomes more like "stop-by-stop." We think, *If I stay focused, I'll figure it out.* But it doesn't happen.

Does it seem like the same thing is often true of men? You find one you like, and the picture on the box looks promising. But when you look inside, there are no instructions. *That's ok*, you think. *He comes preassembled.* You won't need to figure out how to put the pieces together.

But it's not just the instruction manual that's missing. There's also no *operation* manual to describe how he works. You can't find the power button. He turns on all by himself at random times and turns off suddenly when you least expect it. He usually seems to work ok, but there seems to be no way to control him. Most of the time he does what you expect him to do.

Then there are those unexpected times when he doesn't cooperate. You think he'll help with the housework and instead he plops down on a couch and plows through a bag of Cheetos while watching people run around a field on a big screen.

I don't remember signing up for this, you think. You expected a life partner and teammate but feel like somebody programmed him incorrectly—and there's no way to fix him. You're ready to put him back in the box and return him for a different model.

That's when you notice the warning labels on the box that you overlooked:

- "Fragile" (he needs an ego boost to keep functioning)
- "This End Up" (if he gets upset, he doesn't work right)
- "Batteries Not Included" (he runs out of energy at the worst times)

So, what do you do when there's no operation manual? You end up writing your own.

Most women have experienced something similar with the men in their lives. So they talk to each other, trying to figure out what those men are thinking. But without knowing exactly what's going on in a man's mind, it becomes an exercise in futility. They write their own operation manual from their own female frame of reference. It's what they know.

That can be dangerous, because those male differences can be seen as problems to be solved. I've seen a number of books that focus on two approaches:

1. Fixing those differences
2. Coping with those differences

Both of those can be unhealthy. They ignore the fact that differences are *essential* for a relationship to grow and thrive. That's the third option, and the one that lays the foundation for this journey: how to *embrace those differences.*

I know you're eager to start working on those differences. But the best way to explore and embrace our differences is to start with a solid foundation of our similarities. There are more similarities between men and women than there are differences. If we can capitalize on the ways we're alike, we'll be much more inclined to appreciate the ways we're different.

Focusing only on the differences can make it feel like you got a raw deal. It feels like it won't get any better, and you're stuck. When that happens, you feel like you have to take care of yourself and meet your own needs, since your man isn't interested in doing so. You signed up for a relationship but it feels like you're still alone.

That's why it's so important to start with the similarities. Focusing on the many ways we're all alike gives us a balanced perspective of our relationships. The basic needs we have as humans apply to everyone.

Simply stated: the similarities between men and women are really similar. The differences are really different.

The Foundation of Similarities

My son, Tim, was married less than a year ago. The other week I asked him, "So, what have you discovered about marriage that you weren't expecting?"

"How much fun it could be," he replied. "But also how different we are—and how good that is."

I asked him to explain. "In college," he said, "I dated girls that were just like me. I figured that the thing that drew us together was how similar we were. We liked the same things, had the same tastes, and even shared a lot of the same personality traits. I thought that if you were going to find your soul mate, it would look like that."

He continued, "But Lucy and I are total opposites. Everything about her is different, and that's what makes it so much fun. I never know what to expect. And she sees things differently than I do. I think I'm right about something, and she brings a whole different perspective that makes me rethink everything. Everything turns out better when we work together than when we try to see whose idea is right."

I've thought about his answer a lot in the past couple of weeks, and realized the wisdom of my son's perspective. Most of us are drawn to people who think the way we do. It's comfortable and familiar. Those similarities make it easy to connect with others and provide a great place to begin any relationship.

But everybody's unique. People who connect with others through similarities are often split apart by their differences over time. The similarities were comfortable; the differences are uncomfortable. When those differences start to show up, it's easy to focus on them and let them overshadow the similarities. We think the other person has changed, but we've really just hung in there long enough to see their uniqueness leak out.

It's true in every relationship: marriage, business, dating, family, and friendships. We gravitate toward our comfort zones and avoid the uncomfortable. So, in a crowd, I'll hang out with you if you're a lot like me. When you start telling me about the lint collection you keep stored in your refrigerator or your interest in subterranean termite species, it gets a little weird and I excuse myself (unless I share those interests). We start with similarities and divide over differences.

The Home Court Advantage

Similarities provide the "home court advantage" for relationships, whether personal, romantic, casual, or business. So as we study the differences between men and women, we should also take some time to reinforce our similarities. How are we alike? What do we all need?

Look at some of the similarities both men and women have that provide this foundation. To varying degrees, we all need to be:

- *Loved*—we have a place in someone else's heart
- *Respected*—someone admires us for our personal qualities, achievement, or status
- *Needed*—someone has a vacuum in their life that we fill
- *Focused on*—another person is intentional about caring for us

31

- *Noticed*—we capture someone's attention rather than being invisible
- *Valued*—someone would feel a loss if we were not in their life
- *Refreshed*—someone brings a casual lightness into our life
- *Trusted*—another person feels safe in our presence and shares their life openly
- *Listened to*—when we talk, someone wants to understand, not just to reply
- *Encouraged*—others give us fresh strength to continue when ours is lacking
- *Shown commitment*—there's someone who we trust won't give up on us when things get crazy
- *Allowed to dream*—dreaming is risky and creative, and we need someone who doesn't put us down for those wild ideas for the future

There could be more items in this list, but the point is clear. We have a lot more similarities with others than differences, simply by being human.

Imagine how our relationships would thrive if we tried to meet each other's basic needs instead of focusing on our differences. If we were intentional about capitalizing on our similarities, we might not need this book. Meeting the needs all of us share provides the solid foundation that allows us to handle our differences when they arise.

When you're trusted, respected, listened to, and encouraged by someone, how does it feel? What if you could focus on the men in your life with that agenda? By being intentional about building into the lives of others, you set the stage for healthy, effective relationships. Male bosses become real people whom you can relate to instead of feeling like you just have to please. Your co-workers and friends become *people* whom you share life experiences with. The man you're romantic with and your sons are different from you, but you share more in common with them than you might realize.

When differences cause friction, they can take all your energy and focus. "Men are just crazy," you say. "I can't figure them out." It's true, and it can be frustrating. If you're not wrestling with those feelings right now, you may be there soon. It's real, and it's ok.

But on a journey of exploration, we start with our similarities. They're just as real as our differences, and they're critical to keeping our relationships healthy.

Here are several principles we can start with:

1. Similarities are good, and they're comfortable. They draw people together.
2. Differences are good, but they can be uncomfortable. They can push people apart.
3. Healthy relationships come when the similarities aren't forgotten and the differences are celebrated.

The Power of a Comfort Zone

Trish told Jon about a troubling conversation she had with a friend. Jon listened and asked a few questions. A few days later, Trish brought the subject up again, and Jon didn't remember talking about it.

From her perspective, it looked like he was uncaring and insensitive. But Jon didn't feel that way at all and didn't understand what happened. He knew he had hurt her but didn't know why—or what to do about it.

Like Trish and John, we all see life through our own "lenses." We've developed those lenses over a lifetime of experience and found the ones that work best for us. We don't usually question those lenses because everything seems obvious to us when we look through them. But if we assume that everyone has the same lenses that we do, we'll have trouble communicating with others.

Let's focus on understanding others' lenses, not changing them. None of us like to have people trying to "fix" us. We want to be accepted for who we are, even with our idiosyncrasies. When we feel accepted, we feel safe. When we feel safe, we're more likely to make changes on our own.

Men are different from women, but they're not *completely* different. Our similarities provide comfort zones in our relationships where we can be ourselves.

People often say we need to "leave our comfort zones." That's appropriate for goal setting and moving forward in our lives. But in relationships, comfort zones are important. It's not realistic or practical to be *constantly* stretching. The comfort zone is where we live, relax, and regroup. It's where we recharge and gain energy for the next adventure. It's where we are . . . well, *comfortable.*

Exercise is a good analogy. When we lift weights, we push our muscles out of their comfort zone. That exertion is how those muscles grow. But once we're done, those same muscles need time to recover. Growth comes from repeated cycles of exertion and rest. That rest period—the comfort zone—prepares those muscles to be stretched again in the future and builds their capacity for greater work.

In relationships, our similarities provide that comfort zone. That comfort zone should make up the biggest chunk of our relationship. When differences arise, they strain that comfort zone and take us to challenging places. Understanding those differences allows us to move back into our comfort zones. But if we don't understand them, we can get stuck in a constant state of frustration.

The longer we're away from our comfort zone, the less safe we feel. It feels like someone has bolted the door of that comfort zone and we've lost the key.

When I'm on a business trip, I don't get to relax the way I do at home. I'm catching flights, returning rental cars, finding meals on the run, interacting with clients, and speaking in front of groups all day long. Making close flight connections is always a little unnerving, and it's easy to feel exhausted by the time my plane hits the tarmac. I'm almost home, but still have to make the drive back to my house. Pulling into my driveway feels like I've arrived at an oasis in the desert after being in the blazing sun all day. I can finally relax. I've arrived at my comfort zone. That's where I recharge for the next journey.

We All Have "Stuff"

When we minimize our similarities, it's easy to pigeonhole people (especially the opposite gender) and think, *Well, that's just the way they are*. But much of the time, the things that frustrate us don't come from being male or female. They come from the "stuff" we bring with us from our past.

"Stuff" includes those ways we have of handling life that are ineffective. Sometimes it comes from the way we were raised—whether we were nurtured or not, how we were disciplined, or how we were parented (by parents who had their own stuff). Other times, it comes from life experiences, where we've encountered a painful situation and didn't know what to do. We didn't like the way it felt, so we developed walls or strategies to keep from getting hurt again.

We didn't get to pick our parents. We didn't get to choose our socioeconomic status, our place of upbringing, or the experiences that others took us through. We were kids and didn't have the tools to make adult choices. Little by little, we picked up whatever tools were available to us when we needed them.

As we got older, we moved toward adulthood with the tools we had. Some of them worked, some were ineffective, and some were missing. As adults, we still use those tools to negotiate life. Sometimes the tools work well, like well-practiced conversational skills. Sometimes the tools don't do the job, such as when we're trying to negotiate with a person who just won't listen—period. Our tools aren't working and we don't know what else to do. We need new tools but don't know where to find them.

That's "stuff." Stuff refers to the tools we don't have or that don't work—the things that keep us from handling life and relationships.

Everybody has stuff. Men have stuff. Women have stuff.

We start with the similarities, because those things draw us together. Then, when we look at the differences, it's important to determine their source. When you find yourself frustrated by a man, it's important to determine if it's part of his maleness or if it comes from his stuff.

If it's part of his maleness, it won't change. It's best to recognize the reality of it and learn how to respond and deal with it.

If it comes from his stuff, it doesn't have to be permanent. It might be deep-seated, but it's something worth exploring.

A man can get help with his stuff, but he can't change being a man.

All Men Are Not Alike

It's also true that we can't profile men as all being alike. Every time someone says, "All men are (fill in the blank)," the statement becomes invalid. Men are different from women in fairly predictable ways, but every man's differences are unique. One man might be more sensitive while another is not. One man tends to be driven by performance while another is driven by reflection.

As an introvert, I tend to be much more on the reflective side. I don't make decisions quickly, because I find myself exploring all the options first. That sounds good, but it leads to procrastination.

An extrovert might be more spontaneous, taking action without spending a lot of time thinking through the options. They get a ton of stuff done, but their decisions might not always have the best outcomes.

So just as there are similarities and differences between men and women, it's true of men as well. There are a bunch of ways they're alike, and there are ways that each one is unique. When you put their similarities and differences side by side, the similarities win. The differences are relatively few in comparison. It's important to study them, but only after getting a rock-solid view of the similarities.

The journey we're on is to explore the ways in which men are different from women but similar to each other. The strategy is to grasp the basic characteristics that apply to most men in general, then see what each one looks like with each individual man.

Celebrating Differences

I've heard a lot of teaching on this topic suggesting that men need to be either catered to or conquered. Those are dangerous positions that make it tough to build real, healthy relationships.

If men need to be catered to, it suggests that a woman is supposed to please a man. "That's just how men are," the books say. "You have to change and accommodate them." That disrespects both men and women by implying that men are always right and women have to change.

If men need to be conquered, it assumes that their differences are negative. It sets up a battle between the sexes where women need to show their strength to succeed in relationships. That position also disrespects both men and women by assuming that somebody's always right and somebody's always wrong.

The only option that results in healthy relationships is to recognize the reality of those differences and see them as ingredients for an amazing connection. It's more than accepting those differences; it's *celebrating* them.

There's nothing more fascinating than exploring another person. As two people grow, their uniqueness can become a never-ending source of mystery. Ask any couple who has been together for decades, and they'll talk about the new things they're still discovering about each other. They're not in a constant battle for compliance; they're in a partnership to live in *wonder*.

2

What He Wants
You to Know

Your son comes to you and says, "I'm hungry." What do you say?

If you're like most parents, you might respond in one of these ways:

"You're not hungry. You just ate an hour ago."

"We're not stopping for anything. You'll have to wait until we get home."

"Wait until lunchtime."

"You don't need ice cream. You just saw that commercial and it made you want some."

"Here are some carrot sticks. You need something healthy."

It's part of our job as parents to make sure our children get what they need. We've learned from experience that "I'm hungry" can mean a lot of different things. So we get into the habit of saying no when they ask. It's our way of handling nonstop requests.

That's why it's rare for a parent to respond to "I'm hungry" with, "Why, sure. What would you like?" We might decide to say that, but only when we've determined that the unspoken request is legitimate.

Now, your man comes to you and says, "I'm hungry," or "I want you to go to the game with me," or "I'm feeling romantic," or "I just want to stay home today." What do you say? Or even before that, what do you *think*?

He probably grew up like most kids, asking for a ton of things and having his mom say no to most of them. But now he's a man and values his independence. He finds value in being able to make his own choices and has spent most of his life working toward that. It's part of how he's wired.

If you usually find yourself questioning the validity of his requests, you might be doing so out of great motives. You're interested in his well-being and want him to make the right choices. But guess what happens in his brain when you second-guess his requests?

That's right—you just became his mom. And in most adult relationships, that's not a healthy place to go.

That doesn't mean you should automatically do whatever he suggests. After all, he's still a little boy inside who wants everything he sees. But choosing how you address the issue will determine how he responds. If you challenge the logic of his requests without exploring what he's really thinking, he'll feel like he's back in his childhood again. If you want him to respond well, you'll need to start by looking through his lenses.

How do you do that? By responding instead of reacting—asking him to tell you what he's thinking instead of assuming you understand. Instead of saying, "Are you crazy? We've got too much to do around here today to go to the game!" try a different approach: "Which game? What time does it start? You know, that really sounds like a fun time with you. I do have some ideas about what I wanted to get done today, and I was really hoping to make that happen. Can we talk about it, so we can find a way to make it work for both of us?"

The first approach makes a man feel like he's come up against an obstacle, someone telling him he can't do what he wants. The second shows respect for him and allows him to go into problem-solving mode with you, which is what he's good at. It positions you as a team against a problem instead of against each other.

What Other Things Are Men Thinking?

I heard that last scenario from a man who was expressing his frustration with his wife's reactions anytime he wanted to do something. "It feels controlling," he said, "and that's not what a good relationship should look like. Why can't she just talk to me about things instead of pushing her position against mine? I don't need to always get my way, but when she always reacts to my ideas, it feels like I have to fight her on everything."

Over the past year of working on this topic, I've been talking to a lot of men about the subject. One question I've asked often is this: "What do you wish you could tell women that you don't think they know?" Often, they start with a sigh before responding, as if to say, *Wow—that would be great if they knew what we were really thinking.*

It seems like men all have things they want their women to understand, and maybe have tried to tell them. For a variety of reasons, it hasn't gotten through. In most cases, they feel like their women just aren't open to hearing a man's side of things (or she is dismissive when he shares). Some of men's answers to my question relate specifically to marriage, while some relate more to dating. All can be applied to some degree to men in general.

Again, keep in mind that we're talking about quality men who want to do life right and make their relationships healthy but might not know how to go about it. There are men who haven't matured enough to value relationships with women, or have deeper psychological or behavioral issues that need to be dealt with. That's a different issue.

Gentlemen, You May Proceed

I've kept track of the answers my question has gotten and found that there are six broad areas men want to address.

1. How men view their partnerships with women.

Men want a partner, not another mom.

Partners work together toward a common goal. They're not focused on who is right and who is wrong but rather on how they can work together to make something happen. They don't expect the other person to like the same things they like, and they accept them as a whole person rather than trying to change them.

Men are just as committed to that process as women are, maybe even more. They carry it out differently, but the commitment is there. He's vested in you more than he's able to say and wants your relationship to thrive. But in his mind, it has to be a team effort. Here's what various men had to say:

"If you want to work on the relationship, I'll be on board as long as you don't dictate the terms. We need to do it together."

"We're loyal to you and defend you in front of others. We don't talk negatively to our family about you, and we don't want our family members doing it either. We stick up for you. Make sure you're willing to defend us in the same way."

"Don't sign us up for an event without asking. Talk to us first and let us decide. If we don't have a choice, we'll be upset the whole time. If we have a choice, we might do it just to please you."

"Home needs to be a safe place where both of us can go at the end of a hard day. It needs to be the place we want to come to the most, because it's where we're with someone who believes in us and loves us no matter what."

2. How men see their outside relationships.

Men want you to understand their need to connect with other men, and they don't want you to be jealous of other women. Almost all of the men I talked to said the former was a genuine need, and the latter was completely unfounded.

"There's something about hanging out with other guys that feeds our manhood. It doesn't mean we don't want to be with you. But if we spend time with them, it restores that part of us that allows us to bring our best to you."

"When we're with the guys, we don't mind you calling or texting if you need us. But don't do it because you're suspicious or you feel like you have to keep track of us. We'll be ok, and we'll be back."

"When someone flirts with us and it bothers you, talk to us about it. That flirting might feel good to us, but we're with you. If you just get jealous and we haven't done anything to betray you, it feels like you don't trust us."

"Know that we're committed to you and we don't want to cheat on you. We should say it more often, but we think you're beautiful, smart, and clever. What other women have doesn't even begin to match what we have with you."

"When you're jealous, we don't feel respected or trusted. Just because you know someone else who cheated doesn't mean we're going to. That lack of trust eats away at our connection."

3. *What men really think and feel about women.*

Women have more of an impact on men than they realize. Even if it seems like men are distracted by a million different things, almost everything they do is to get their woman's attention.

"We want you to be impressed with us. We need you to enjoy having us around. Our 'ok-ness' depends on how you feel about us. Give us the benefit of the doubt when we don't do it right. We're trying, and we're doing it for you."

"We have deep emotions, but we've been brought up not to show them. They're in there. They're often about you, and little things remind us of you when we're not with you."

"When you smile at us, it makes our whole day. Seriously. And if we can't make you smile, the day is heavier."

"We really want to make you happy. You probably need to tell us what that looks like, but we really want it to happen."

"We're not always thinking about sex. It's important to us, but it's nothing like they make it sound on TV. We tend to focus on one thing at a time. Sex is one of those things, and we need it often to function. But it's not the only thing."

"Don't look for hidden meaning when we say things. We're not that complicated. If we tell you we like the way you look today, it doesn't imply that we don't like the way you look on other days. Take it at face value as a compliment, and say thanks."

"We express our love through our actions more than words. Pay attention to those little things we do, because they're on purpose. Most of the little things we do are to make your life a little easier. That's our way of loving you."

4. What men think about women's looks.

This question turned out to be pretty straightforward. Women often obsess about their looks, but men think they look great anytime.

"You're a lot prettier than you think. We really believe that."

"Accept it when we tell you you're beautiful. Stop responding by putting yourself down. We're just stating what we believe to be true, and you're saying we're wrong. That's frustrating."

"We don't like a lot of makeup. We like it when you make yourself up when we go out, but we seriously love the way you look at home with no makeup at all. We fell in love with the real you, not the decorated you."

"Your attitude has more to do with how attractive you are than anything else. A confident, playful woman is hard for a man to resist."

"You worry about sags and scars and cellulite. When you're naked, we're not focused on that. We have other things that distract us. We're just enjoying you."

"Take care of yourself. We want you to relax at home, but it's important to us that you take effort to look nice for us sometimes. That doesn't mean fancy clothes and makeup, because you need to be comfortable. When you dress nice to go out but *always* look shabby at home, we still love you—but we feel like we're getting the leftovers."

5. How men communicate.

Communication is the key to an effective relationship. If we don't see through each other's filters, men and women can really get frustrated when their differences aren't taken into consideration.

"We have no idea what you want. Don't drop hints—we won't get them. Just tell us what you want—we really want to know."

"If we're silent, we're probably thinking. Or we might be upset, but we don't want to blurt out anything that might hurt you. Or we might not be thinking at all."

"Don't bring up things from the past during an argument. Keep it in the past, and stay with the current situation."

"If something we say comes out wrong, it doesn't mean there's something deep inside that came out under pressure. It just means we said it wrong."

"It's easier for us to feel close to you when we're doing something together than when we're just sitting and talking."

"Your words impact us more than you'll ever know. If you compliment us in the smallest way, it will carry us for days. Tell us we look nice, and we'll wear that same shirt every time we can."

"We can't always read your facial expressions. The only way we know you're hurt is if you tell us. If you want us to put away the dishes, don't try to look tired so we'll pick up on it. Ask us to put the dishes away.

We'd love to do it because it helps you out. But we just won't figure it out on our own."

"We can't be your girlfriend. You have girlfriends to be that for you. We can only provide what we have to give."

"Give us time to think when we're having a conversation. We need to process what you've said before we can respond."

6. What men need.

Men consistently said that women don't know what men need, because it's different from what women need. So when women discover what those needs are, it's important to recognize that they are genuine.

"We need to be admired in all areas of life. Tell us when you notice us doing things well."

"We need to feel desired by you. If we don't, it shakes our confidence. All it takes is a little playful flirting, and we melt."

"We love it when you rest your head on our shoulder."

"The biggest compliment you can give is that you feel safe with us. It satisfies our protective instinct."

"We're insecure. We need affirmation that we're ok. Often."

"If we sense that you're in our court and you encourage us, we feel like we can do anything. Make us feel that way, and we'll always have your back."

"We need to feel useful to you. When you ask us to do things for you, it fulfills our sense of responsibility."

"We want to be your hero. If you convince us that it's true, we'll do anything for you."

Replace Assumptions with Communication

There's one simple truth that summarizes this chapter: men think differently than women. The only way women will discover how men think is to talk to them about it.

Over the years, my wife and I have gotten better at communicating exactly what we need. It's not natural and it's not perfect, but we're getting better.

When we moved into our current house eight years ago, we had a lot of remodeling to do. We painted, removed partitions, scraped ceilings, and replaced windows. We worked for months on those things . . . and then realized that we didn't have the money to do everything we wanted.

Replacing the carpet was on the list, but we postponed it until most of the other work was done. We didn't paint the baseboards in our guest room because we figured we'd do it at the same time we did the carpet. But things got tight, and we still haven't replaced that carpet. It's pretty bad, but we're not going to spend money we don't have.

A few weeks ago, I noticed that those baseboards had never been painted. It made the room look unfinished, but we'd gotten used to it. Neither of us even thought about it, though I'm sure our guests have wondered.

I had a couple of days off work last week, so I decided to paint those baseboards. It will still be a while before we replace the carpet, but at least the room will look finished. I cleaned them, taped around the carpet, and carefully applied two coats of paint. When I put the room back together it looked like a different room.

In the past, I would have waited for Diane to notice and then say something. Sometimes she'd go for days without noticing, and I'd start feeling hurt that she wasn't appreciating my effort. But I've learned to take a more direct approach.

When she came home from work, I said, "Let me know when you have a few spare minutes to come in the guest room and ooh and aah over the baseboards I painted."

She said, "Ok—give me three minutes."

Three minutes later she grabbed my hand and walked into the guest room. She looked slowly around and playfully said, "Ooh!" A few seconds later she said, "Aah!" Then she followed it up with a genuine compliment: "This looks like a totally different room. It just lightens the whole thing up. You did a really nice job in here. Thanks!"

It was direct. It was fun. And it gave me a sense of respect from her that has lasted for several days. Why? Because I told her exactly what I needed.

And the best part? I got to be her "baseboard hero."

I live for that. And your man does too.

PART 2

How He Thinks

The first time my wife and I visited Hawaii, we were caught up in the beauty of the experience. It was one of those weeks where we were in love with life, each other, and our surroundings. The backdrop of the intense island colors captured our emotions like a photograph captures one's vision.

Returning home felt like the end of Christmas, when you have to take down the decorations and return to normal life. It had been such a great experience that we didn't want to let it go. So we talked about landscaping our yard with tropical plants to re-create the experience. When things got rough, we could escape to paradise by walking out the back door.

We never really did that, except we brought home a plumeria. It's the tree that produces the unique, fragrant flowers used in making traditional leis. It looked like a foot-long dead twig, and we were supposed to stick it in the ground and it would grow.

It worked. Sort of.

Over the next few years it grew a bit, formed a couple of branches, and produced six or seven flowers each year. We could smell them if we got really close, but it certainly didn't fill the yard with fragrance. It never did well in our climate—at least not as well as it did in Hawaii.

We realized later that we were trying to treat it the way we did our other plants and expecting it to flourish. If we had studied its unique characteristics and needs, our expectations would have been different. It could have been a great part of our garden with the proper care and feeding.

Men are like that. They think differently than women. If a woman assumes that her man has the same thought processes she does, she'll always be disappointed in the results. If she wants him to reach his full potential, she needs to know what goes on inside his head. With that knowledge, she'll be able to make choices that help him—and their relationship—thrive.

3

Gray Matters

In the early days of television Westerns, it was easy to tell the good guys from the bad guys. The good guys wore white hats, and the bad guys wore black hats.

Over time, people wanted more mystery in those shows. So the producers would mix it up once in a while. You thought you knew who the good guys and bad guys were because of their hats. But suddenly the guy with the white hat turned out to be the villain. The guy with the black hat was the one who put the villain in jail.

Today, movie and television plots have become much more involved and sophisticated. From the beginning of the show, we watch the characters and make assumptions about them based on how they look or act. One person looks relaxed and sincere, dresses comfortably, and seems like someone you'd like to meet for coffee. Another never smiles, looks sideways out of squinted eyes, and just has an aura of deceit. You wouldn't want to meet that guy or gal in a dark alley.

But as the plot develops, the friendly character turns out to be a charmer who carries out a treacherous scheme. The suspicious one is revealed to be the hero who is committed to bringing the other to justice.

It's human nature to profile others based on their appearance. We form opinions from the first few minutes of an encounter then are surprised when that person doesn't live up to our expectations. If the good guy turns out to be a bad guy, we're embarrassed because we couldn't "size them up" accurately.

I once heard a speaker suggest that we form an impression of someone in the first four minutes of a conversation. Once we decide if they're the good guy or the bad guy, our impression tends to stick. If we feel positively toward someone, they can do something really shady and we'll give them the benefit of the doubt. *They're such a good person*, we think. *That must be an isolated incident.* It will take repeated incidents for us to admit that we were wrong. If we feel negatively toward someone after four minutes, and they do something good, we think, *That was a fluke. They're a bad person, so that was out of character.* It takes repeated "good" actions to convince us that we're not seeing them accurately.

I think the basic concept is accurate. But that speaker went on to teach people how to fake it for four minutes, saying, "If you can fake it for four minutes, you can get anybody on your side." I wasn't overly excited about that application, but I got the basic point: right or wrong, we form opinions of others fairly quickly.

Profiling Men

Wouldn't it be great if the high-quality guys always wore white hats and the low-integrity guys wore black hats? But we're not living in a Western movie. It's more like we're carrying out the plots of modern-day movies. You try to figure men out, but they often fail to live up to your expectations.

You meet the man of your dreams. He's sensitive, he wants to spend time with you, he listens, he calls, and he takes the initiative in the relationship. He's not like the stereotypes you've always heard about men. He's different. He's probably not perfect, but he seems pretty close.

He's wearing the white hat.

Sometime later, you're going through a tough situation with a co-worker. You're anxious to tell him about it, because he's always listened to you intently. But this time is a little different. He seems distracted. Before you finish talking, he says, "Well, here's the problem . . . and here's what you should do about it."

Hmmm. That seemed out of character from what you've decided about him, because he's wearing the white hat. So you give him the benefit of the doubt. *He's just tired,* you tell yourself. *He's had a rough couple of days.*

But those things happen more and more often. He doesn't listen as intently as before. His work seems to take more of his focus, and you get less. He's not as intentional about pursuing you as he did in the past. If he's watching TV, you can't get his attention for more than a few seconds. He doesn't pick up on your moods the way he did before. When you're upset, he doesn't even notice, and seems surprised when you tell him.

You're starting to notice a few smudges and stains on the white hat that you didn't notice before. You're also wondering if the stereotypes you've heard about men are true. Maybe you were wrong in thinking he was different. Maybe he's not the man of your dreams, after all.

What's really happening is that you've done what we all do: profile someone based on first impressions. It's human nature. When it's a positive profile, we feel safe. When it's negative, we put up our guard to protect ourselves. It's natural, and we all do it.

The problem comes when we look at someone through our own "lenses" and assume that they have those same lenses.

Let's say a woman observes a man watching sports on television (a stereotype, but common). She says something to him, and he grunts, "Uh-huh." After the game is over, he doesn't even remember the conversation. She feels that if she was the one watching the game and someone talked to her, she would stop watching, engage in the conversation, and then go back to the game. It just makes sense, and it shows common courtesy. That's her lens for that particular situation. It's how she thinks, so it seems like common sense to her.

So when a man doesn't do the same thing, her view through her lenses tells her that he's being rude and inconsiderate. *Why is that game so important that he ignores me?* she thinks. *Don't I matter to him more than sports?*

In reality, he probably doesn't feel like he's ignoring her at all. She means more to him than sports ever will. But he's operating from a different mindset. He's thinking like a man, not a woman. He's thinking, *This is a great game. They're just about to score, and everything is riding on the next couple of plays. I know she wants something, and I'll give her my full attention as soon as it's over. But this is the most exciting part!* Male brains function differently than female brains. A woman can focus on multiple things at a time, while a man gives his entire attention to his current task.

That's the problem with profiling. It makes assumptions based on our own lenses, not the lenses of the other person. To see others accurately, we need to recognize that they might have different lenses. It doesn't mean those lenses are wrong; they're just different.

What Happens in a Male Brain

So, what's really going on inside a man's head? What does he see through his lenses?

There are biological differences between the brains of men and women that help us understand why we respond and react differently. Without getting into deep scientific or medical explanations, let's take a little tour inside his head.

You might have heard that men's brains tend to be larger than women's brains. If so, you probably heard it from a man. He wanted you to know his brain was bigger, implying that he was smarter as well. You weren't convinced—and you shouldn't be.

Most studies show that, as a group, men's brains *are* bigger. But as a group, men's bodies generally tend to be a little bigger than women's too. So it's unfair to use that as the basis for assuming he's smarter.

Here's what's interesting: there are certain parts of a man's brain that do tend to be larger, and that's true of women's brains as well. Both men and women tend to operate from those larger parts of their brains, which influence their choices, attitudes, and behaviors.

You've probably heard the brain referred to as "gray matter." That's because if you look at the human brain, it tends to look fairly gray in color. When someone is thinking clearly, we say, "That's the way to use your gray matter."

Men have more gray matter than women. In fact, they have around six times as much gray matter. It's full of what we call *neurons*, and it's the brain's processing center. Men do most of their thinking with that gray matter. If you want to impress the guy in your life, tell him you discovered that he has six times more gray matter than you do. You can guess what his reaction will be.[1]

But that's not all you need to tell him.

The brain also has what we call "white matter." That consists of the connections between the neurons—the links that pull it all together and transmit signals back and forth in the gray matter. Women have about *ten times* more white matter than men do. That means that women's brains are much more complicated in how they're structured, and they use that network to think faster than men. They make connections between different parts of the brain more easily because of that white matter.[2]

What Does It All Mean?

This means that men and women can work on the same problem or complete the same task but use different parts of their brains to get there.

We hear a child's laughter, see an over-the-top sunset, or smell rain in the desert. Those signals get sent to a part of the brain called the *limbic system*. That's where emotions start, and they get handled by a control center called the *amygdala*. (You don't have to remember that. If you're a woman, you probably will. If you're a man, it's already gone.)

Those brain differences mean that women and men handle those signals and emotions differently.

In general, emotions tend to be less enjoyable for men, and could be a little confusing. They're not sure what to do with them. That's why they choose movies with more action than emotion. It's easier and more natural for them to use all that gray matter to solve a problem, and action movies allow them to do exactly that.

Women often choose dramas and story line movies that explore relationships. Part of a woman's brain that's bigger is called the *hippocampus*. Its job is to remember details of an event when there's emotion involved. That's why a woman might remember specific details of a meaningful event that took place five years ago, including the conversation, the decorations, what people were wearing, and the emotions she felt at the event.

A man is lucky if he remembers the event at all. It doesn't mean he's forgetful. It just means his brain works differently.[3]

That's one of the most significant differences between men and women from a biological perspective. Men tend to think with one part of their brain at a time. It gives them the ability to focus on something, usually at the exclusion of everything else.

When a man stares at a television, his brain is disengaged from everything else happening around him. In fact, one study found that the brain scan of a man watching television was exactly the same as when he stares at a campfire for hours at a time. There's not much happening.

Women's brains are characterized by connections. Whatever they're thinking about is connected to everything else in their brain. They don't take many mental naps, and their brain activity is still in gear when they're at rest. That's why they can hear a baby cry while they're sleeping and most men can sleep right through it.

When relaxed, a woman's mental activity swirls around in the part of the brain that deals with feelings and emotions. A man's restful mind settles less in those emotional sections and more in the "fight or flight" areas. When they sense danger, a man tends to *act* first, then *think*, then *feel*. Women tend to *feel* first, then *think*, then *decide* on what action to take.

As we've said before, not everyone fits those exact patterns. Every person is unique and carries his or her own unique characteristics into every relationship. You or your man might be just the opposite. But in general, men tend to lean one direction while women lean another.

Does Upbringing Matter?

Some people feel that these characteristics come from a person's upbringing and environment. A boy might get more roughhousing from a parent where a girl would receive more tenderness. Boys might be taught that certain emotions are unmanly, so they learn to hide them. They could also be given different opportunities than girls as they grow up.

There's definite influence from our upbringing. We didn't get to choose where we were born, who our parents were, what our environment was like, or whether or not we were nurtured and loved. We were given (or not given) the tools we use to handle life and didn't get to decide which ones we received. So, of course, our upbringing influences our behavior as adults.

But we can't overlook the reality of those biological differences, especially in the way the brain works. It's futile to fight about how men and women relate, as if the other person is just being stubborn. In most cases the issue is that men are simply operating the way their brain is wired.

Take testosterone, for example. It's a hormone that men tend to have a lot of, while women have little. In fact, men usually have about six times more testosterone than women. When a male baby is in the womb, he gets a "testosterone bath" at about the eight-week mark. That's when the male characteristics begin to form, both physically and mentally.

When boys reach about the age of six, that testosterone causes them to sort out a pecking order with friends. Listen to their conversations, and they're pulling themselves up and putting others down. They typically develop characteristics of aggressiveness and competition. High testosterone serves a person well if they're doing one-on-one sports and competition, where lower testosterone enables them to participate effectively in team situations.

My daughter, Sara, has always been amazed at how different her five-year-old son, Marco, is than his two older sisters. "He's all boy," she says, "and he's been that way since day one. The girls just played differently. He's rougher, more physical and competitive, louder, and he wants to win. He's just simply interested in different things than the girls were."

That isn't environmental; he's been that way since birth. That testosterone seems to be doing its job.

This brain chemistry changes as males get older. Men tend to be more competitive when they're young and more cooperative as they mature. As men move through life, their priorities often shift toward relationships and community.

I've noticed that as I've gotten older, my interests have changed. Years ago, I was trying to prove myself and build a career. I had friends, but they weren't the highest priorities on my mental list. But now I'm finding that my friends are becoming more important to me than before. I still want to be successful and strive to make a difference. But I don't need to be rich and famous; I'm more interested in having some real relationships with people who matter to me, especially my wife and kids and grandkids.

I've also known men who were tough as nails when they were younger, but have softened with compassion as they matured. They're still men; they just have different priorities and ways of expressing their maleness.

Capitalizing on the Differences

If a woman tries to change the things in her man that drive her crazy, she's probably setting herself up for frustration. As Robert Heinlein said, "Never try to teach a pig to sing; it wastes your time and it annoys the pig."[4]

There are some things about men that come from their maleness, and some things that come from their choices. The key to your sanity is to understand and discern the difference between the two.

It's a three-step process:

1. Determine what, exactly, he is doing that frustrates you.
2. Ask yourself if it is something that is just part of his being a man (such as the way he processes information). If so, don't try to change it. Learn to accept the reality of it, and decide how to capitalize on it.

3. If not, is it something that he has simply developed as a pattern, habit, or behavior (such as the way he withdraws from conflict)? Then it's negotiable. It won't change by pointing it out as a problem. Change comes through influence and trust. When a man feels that he's in a safe relationship that has meaning to him, he'll be more inclined to work on the behaviors that are so challenging to you.

The inner workings of a man's brain are real. In fact, those realities are the exact things that can create the greatest connections in your relationship. His interest in sports and action films doesn't mean he's not interested in you or in romance. In fact, romance is usually a key factor in most action films.

Yesterday was Easter Sunday. The pastor began his sermon by saying, "Today we're going to talk about love stories. Turn to the person next to you and tell them what your favorite love story movie is."

I know that, as a guy, I'm supposed to like action films and riveting dramas. I was trying to think of a movie that combined those with a love story, and figured it would have to be something like *Braveheart* or *Casablanca* or something with a rugged man becoming the hero to his woman. But I had to be honest, because my wife already knew the answer: I've always been a sucker for *Sleepless in Seattle.* Maybe not the whole movie, but the beginning (where Tom Hanks describes his love for his late wife and relates tenderly to his son) and the end (where he meets Meg Ryan on top of the Empire State Building).

Fortunately, the pastor said, "Men, if you said *Titanic*, you still get to keep your 'man card.'"

Yesterday was also my son's birthday, so we ended the day by seeing *Fast and Furious 7*. That's about as manly as they get. And guess what? The focal point of that movie was a man wanting to be the hero for his woman.

It's interesting that while men are drawn to action and adventure films, they love the ones that have a rough, macho man who becomes tender with the love of his life. It's a common theme in movies, and it's a common theme for most men: *we want to be your hero.*

That's hardwired. It's tucked away in a man's brain.

That's the place to start in understanding men—knowing what happens in their brain and why it happens.

4

Men Are Just Tall Boys

"Mommy, watch! Daddy, watch!"

When kids are little, their parents probably hear that phrase a hundred times a day. Anytime kids learn how to do the slightest thing, they want their parents to notice and respond. They figure out how to do an unwieldy somersault: "Mommy, watch!" They blow bubbles for the first time: "Daddy, watch!" They go higher than ever on the swing: "Mommy—Daddy—watch!"

It doesn't stop with watching; they also want participation. "Push me," they say on the swing. "Come with me," they shout as they go exploring. "Read to me . . . sit with me . . . can I come too?" They're learning about life and want to share every moment of it. They want their parents to be there for them and with them. They want them to celebrate their accomplishments and cheer their attempts and encourage their progress and share their joy.

They want to be known. They want to be loved. They want to be respected.

My kids are grown up now, and nothing has changed. Though their need looks different, and they're much more sophisticated about it, they still crave recognition and approval.

It matters to them that they matter to us.

Guess what? That man in your life? Nothing has changed. He wants to be known. He wants to be loved. He wants to be respected . . . by you. He might get kudos from a lot of other people at work and in life, but none of it matters as much as what he gets from you.

The Birth of Needs

Everyone is born with that need to be valued—to matter to somebody else. If kids are raised in a healthy, loving environment, they get the message that says, "I'm glad you're here. You have value just because you're you." If they are raised in a toxic environment, they hear messages that say, "You don't matter."

When boys are little, those needs are real. If they're not met, the drive to fulfill those needs doesn't go away. So they look for alternative ways of having them met. Sometimes those ways might be harmful, but they stick with them if they work. Those techniques are all they know, and they are better than having unsatisfied needs.

It's like the scenario where a woman stays in an abusive dating relationship. Everyone can see that it's dangerous and toxic and it's destroying her sense of self-worth. "You need to get out of that relationship," they tell her. But she's afraid that if she leaves she won't find someone else who wants her. So she stays in that harmful situation because she's afraid of change (or afraid that an alternative wouldn't be any better).

A man finds value from good early experiences and feels devalued if he has bad experiences. In either case, it's his reality. It's all he knows, and it was scripted in his mind very early in his life. He's hardwired to seek value throughout his life.

Jerry was one of those boys. His dad didn't know how to have a real relationship with him, so their connection centered on sports and his dad coached his teams as he went through school. They memorized statistics of players of their favorite teams and went to games together. At home their conversations centered on the day's statistics, and the sports channel was always on in the background.

As an adult, Jerry wanted a closer relationship with his dad. But his dad didn't know how to do it. They could talk about sports, but Jerry longed for his dad to ask him about his family, his life, and his other interests. He wanted to know that his dad cared about who he was. He tried to reach out to his dad, buying him gifts or going to games together. He wanted his dad to tell him that he was proud of him. But no matter what Jerry did, there was no real change.

That's not an isolated story. Adult men have the same basic needs they did when they were little. If those needs weren't met by their parents while they were growing up, they have a drive to make it happen later in life. Often, a parent dies without a son gaining the approval he seeks, and it impacts his choices for the rest of his life.

Study the Child

From a brain perspective, men are pretty simple. Watch what goes on in the head of a boy, and you'll probably have a good idea what goes on when he becomes an adult. He gets more sophisticated in his approach, but the basic needs are still there.

I once heard that you can observe the basic personality of a six-year-old and get a pretty accurate idea of what they'll be like as an adult. (If you have a six-year-old, you're probably starting to panic.) By the time they hit age six, they've figured out how people perceive them, made decisions about how much value they have, and have developed their basic tools for negotiating life. They have decided whether other people can be trusted or not, sensed if they have integrity, and watched what adults do that seems to work for them in life. They've determined what their reality is and have made choices about how to function.

If that's true, we could probably work from the opposite direction. Study an adult man carefully—discover his motivations, his temperament, the way he relates to others, and the amount of trust he has in relationships—and you can probably get a good idea of what he was like at age six. In fact, that would make an interesting conversation with older adults who knew him at that age. There's a good chance you'll recognize that boy in your man.

I have three grandchildren, currently ages five, eight, and eleven. It's fascinating to study them and watch them grow and develop. I don't know how they'll turn out, but I find myself projecting them into the future, picturing them as adults with their current temperaments. I'm guessing I'll still recognize some of those childhood characteristics as they mature.

In a sense, men are just tall boys. That doesn't mean change is hopeless. Anyone can change if they have the intrinsic motivation and the support of others. But it's tough, and it's not guaranteed. It's hard to make changes in our own life, and it's just as hard for others to change themselves.

One of the best ways to begin understanding the man in your life is to look at the little boy inside. His basic needs are still there, and they still need to be met. When you see behaviors and attitudes that seem unreasonable or hard to understand, they might be symptoms of an unmet need.

Why Men Don't Change

My wife's parents live in Bakersfield, California, and have a cabin they built in the mountains about ninety minutes away. To get there, you have to drive through a steep, winding canyon. The Kern River at the bottom is filled with house-sized boulders, producing breathtaking rapids. Most of it is too dangerous for swimming or even whitewater rafting, but some people still try. In fact, there's a sign at the entrance of the canyon with changeable numbers that says, "351 people have lost their lives in this river" in an attempt to keep people out. Every year, we see the number go up. The thing that makes it dangerous is exactly what makes it so spectacular.

That river started as a trickling stream thousands of years ago. Over time, it began to cut a groove in the earth. That groove became the banks of a stream, then a river, then a canyon. It's the same river. But given enough time, its impact deepens.

Sound like your man? He's fascinating and inviting, but sometimes you feel like you're negotiating the rapids in your relationship. Like the steep canyon that has been formed by the river, the choices he made as a boy have carved the shape of his manhood. His adult behavior isn't new; it started a long time ago and formed who he has become. Every time a man repeats a behavior, it cuts the canyon just a little bit deeper. When you enter a relationship with a man, you're experiencing everything he has been in the past. And the older a man gets, the more those patterns are established.

More than just habits he's developed, those patterns are his operating system. Over the years, they have become the way he negotiates life. Where did those patterns come from? There are two primary sources, environment and genetics.

Environment is a big influence, especially the people who were in a boy's life as he was growing up. For example, a boy looks to his parents to have his needs met and learn about life. Their presence or absence shapes that boy's beliefs, attitudes, and choices about how life works. It determines the initial path the river takes when it's just a trickle. But once the tiniest groove has been established, the river begins to stay in that path.

There are siblings, extended family members, neighbors, and friends who are part of that environment as well. A boy doesn't realize he's watching those other people, but he's observing how life works by seeing how they handle it. There's no formal training course or an initiation event that turns him into a man.

He wants to know how he's supposed to do life, so he looks for a role model to watch and emulate. If he doesn't get a good role model from his parents, he'll look at sports figures, successful celebrities, or older boys to pick up those skills. Sometimes he even engages in high-risk activities to find that sense of achievement and worth, or he might disengage his emotions and just ignore that need.

A man can change what he learned from his early environment, but it won't be easy—any more than it is easy for a river to take a new path. We can stand at the top of the canyon and dig a new channel, but it's going to be tough to convince that river to try something new. In the same way, it's easier to learn to understand what brought your man to his current place in life than to hope for an totally new direction.

The second factor is *genetics*. The hormones that determine his maleness are hardwired in. He is born with unique characteristics that make him male rather than female, and trying to change them would be like turning an oak tree into an orange tree. We might love the shade the oak tree provides, but we get tired of raking the leaves. Yet wishing for fruit on an oak tree is an exercise in futility. A better way to avoid frustration would be to take a class on how to turn oak leaves into mulch.

Vertical Relationships

When we talked earlier about the physiological structure of a man's brain, we learned that women have more connective tissue between different parts of their brains than men. Men have more "gray matter," so they tend to compartmentalize their thinking, while women tend to make connections.

In relationships, women tend to think *horizontally*. Relating to others is a matter of connection, and they're focused on the dynamics of relationships between different people. Watch a group of small girls playing together, and they'll often play "house" or "school," where each one plays a specific role in the story. One might be the mom or teacher and assign roles for the others to play. The conversation centers around group dynamics, making sure everyone is happy or engaged.

Men, however, tend to view relationships *vertically*. Put a man in a group, and he'll subconsciously study where he ranks in the pecking order. Watch a group of boys playing together, and it's all about competition and "I can do that better" and who gets to be the leader. They're constantly jockeying for position, comparing abilities or intelligence or status. They aren't very experienced at it, so they'll often compare the people they're connected to. "My dad can beat up your dad," they'll brag.

That competitive spirit isn't a character flaw; it's part of his brain. It's part of his drive to succeed and be on top in most situations of life. It's that drive that makes him channel his energy and resources to compete for the woman he cares most about.

Guys want to be number one, which is why they don't ask for help when doing things. They don't ask for directions because doing so puts them in a position of admitting they can't find a location on their own. (Of course, nowadays technology allows them to get directions on their own without another person involved.)

My friend Al is a seasoned woodworker. He lives about half a mile from me and has just about every tool imaginable. "Don't ever go out and buy a tool when you need one," he told me once. "If you need it, I probably have it. You can just borrow mine."

My wife was with me when he said that, and she remembered it. Every few months after that, I would be working on a project at home and not have the tool I needed. In my mind, the obvious solution was to go buy the tool I needed. I would then have it in the future, when I might need it again.

Diane would say, "Would Al have that tool? Why don't you just go borrow it from him?" I knew she was right, but I always felt irritated. I didn't have a good excuse for not asking Al for help. But if I didn't buy the tool, I might need it again in the future—which would mean I'd have to ask Al for help again.

A couple of times I went to his garage and we worked together on a project, using both his tools and his expertise. We had a great time. But if I needed to do it again, I would find myself looking for another way to do it. Sometimes I felt guilty and prideful for my unwillingness to ask for help. My wife couldn't understand why I didn't make the call when I needed something. After all, it just made sense, right?

But that's because she's looking at my vertical perspective through her horizontal perspective.

This doesn't mean I shouldn't seek out help from others. But the place to start is to recognize the reality of a man's vertical perspective. I'll ask for help, but it's not my first in-clination. I have a basic desire to be competent on my own, and that's how it plays out.

It's a cliché, but it's accurate: *it's a guy thing.*

The Drive to Win

When I first started studying this competitive side of a man's brain, I wasn't convinced. I never played sports in school and have only developed an interest in sports because of my kids. My son-in-law loves ice hockey, has season tickets for our local NHL team, and has spread that virus to his entire family.

Even his youngest son, five-year-old Marco, will sit on the couch with me watching the game, providing colorful commentary the whole time about players and stats and rankings.

So I figured this trait didn't apply to me. *I'm not all that competitive*, I convinced myself. But the more I thought about it, the more I realized that I'm just competitive about different things. It's more subtle, but just as real.

> When I'm stuck in slow-moving traffic, I find myself scanning the other lanes to see if there's a way to get ahead. I'm unsettled when I'm in the back of the pack instead of the front.
>
> At work, we have a ranking system based on client satisfaction. A number of times I've been number one in the country, and it feels good. This year I slipped to number two. The guy who took the top spot is a great friend and deserved it. But I find myself driven to "up my game" to recapture that position next year.
>
> When the rankings of my books on Amazon are high, I feel confident. When they're low, it's stifling. I have a number of friends who are authors, and I have made a personal vow to never check the rankings of their books. It messes with my head if I do, because I look at myself (and them) differently depending on where my books rank compared to theirs.

I've found that I'm not alone. Men subconsciously watch the rankings of their relationships the way they study the standings of their favorite sports team. Relationships are important, but in the male mind they're trumped by perceived status and position.

Channeling the Beast

That vertical perspective explains our previous discussion—why men usually prefer action movies to romantic ones. Action films are about who's conquering another person or a situation. Romantic ones are about connection, which fits the horizontal perspective most women have. That doesn't mean men don't care about romance; they just view it differently. If my wife and I are choosing a movie to watch, her first choice isn't usually my first choice. But once the romantic movie starts, I'm fine with it. I enjoy it, but not the way I do something with more action.

If a woman takes the time to watch an action film with her man, she'll probably recognize that there's usually some type of love story in the middle that captures the male mind. Why does the hero go to such great lengths to come out on top? To capture the heart of his woman.

So it's not an either-or situation. The more a woman recognizes how that male mind works, the easier it will be to recognize why he makes the choices he does. It's not because he's a jerk; it's because he's male.

It started when he was a little boy, and it hasn't changed. He just got taller.

5

Man on a Mission

On January 15, 2009, US Airways Flight 1549 hit a flock of birds and ended up landing in the Hudson River. In the mind of the average citizen, it was a remarkable—even miraculous—achievement. Commercial flights are supposed to land on a runway, not a river. But this time, it was different. Every passenger survived, thanks to the skill of one man.

Before that event, Chesley Sullenberger was known as the captain. After the event, he was known by a new title: *hero*. It wasn't a description he sought, and he downplayed it to the media. He often said, "I was just doing my job. It's what I was trained to do." That self-effacing perspective added an adjective to his new title: *humble hero*.

It was true and well deserved. His calm response to the emergency saved the lives of 155 people. The world was watching, and admiring, and grateful. The media found a new focal point for millions of people who were starved for a genuine hero.

But there was another phenomenon taking place in the hearts of men everywhere. They were justifiably grateful and proud of "Captain Sully" and his performance. They shared the amazement at the captain's cool response and precise actions under pressure. They were moved by the successful outcome. But deep inside, they were thinking, *I wish it could have been me bringing that plane in.*

It might not have even reached the level of conscious thought, but it was there. It's a drive that's tucked away inside every man—the drive to make a difference. It's not a learned response; it's a universal characteristic. Men want to be the ones who excel under pressure, make the right choices, and bring resolution to a tough situation. They want to save the day.

That's another reason men are drawn to action movies. Our favorite scenario is when people are oppressed and there seems to be no hope for them to escape their situation. Then a hero begins to rise through the ranks. It's usually an ordinary guy who has passion and conviction and possesses a deep sense of the injustice surrounding him. He tries to suggest options, but people discourage him from every angle.

Finally, he realizes that if anything is going to happen, he's going to have to step out of his comfort zone and take a stand. He takes risks and capitalizes on his strength and wisdom and leads the people to victory.

He conquers. He wins. He makes a difference. In the end, he has the admiration of everyone around him. He's a hero. When men watch those types of movies, they're living vicariously through those characters. They're saying, "I want to be *that* guy."

Men are wired for conquering. When there's a challenge, they want to solve it. When there's an insurmountable issue, they want to find a way through. When someone says, "It's impossible!" they think, *Yeah? Just watch me.*

But My Guy Isn't Like That!

You might be thinking, *I don't know if I buy that. The guys I know aren't trying to change the world. They're playing video games for hours at a time, or watching sports, or working on their car. I don't see much of a conquering spirit in them.*

Actually, it's there. Look at the video games he's playing; they usually involve a tough character at war against great odds. Watching sports? Whether it's football or Frisbee, he wants to be the one to throw the winning pass. Car repair often involves solving a problem that's eluding him, and he'll be frustrated until he can figure it out. When he does, he feels more satisfaction than you can imagine.

Here's a simple observation: guys want to make a difference. They watch the Captain Sullys of the world. They see the men who pull someone from a burning building, who rush to an accident scene to rescue a trapped passenger, or who disarm a gunman during a bank robbery. They want to be that kind of hero.

But there's a problem. In all those cases, no one planned on being a hero; it just happened. Captain Sully didn't wake up that day and say, "I wonder if this will be the day I lose my engines and land on a river and save a bunch of lives." No one knew the building would burn; it just happened, and the hero was nearby and reacted. The accident occurred and someone needed help, and the hero was conveniently in the next car. No one goes looking for a bank robbery, but people make choices when they end up in one.

Often, they're heroes of convenience.

Most men believe that if they found themselves in those situations, they would make the heroic choice. At least, they hope they would. But they also realize that situations like that are pretty rare. As much as they want to be the hero, they don't have the opportunity.

So what do they do? They look for smaller, more predictable situations where they can be the conqueror. It might be a video game, a broken faucet, or a resistant customer they want to do business with. It could be a golf game, a tough traffic situation, or a steak that needs to be grilled to perfection. It could be any problem in their life that needs solving. When they find the solution, they get to be a mini-hero and they're satisfied for the moment.

How Heroes Grow

Kevin Leman's *The Birth Order Book* describes the unique characteristics of a firstborn child versus a lastborn child. He charts a clear path for parents to understand why the firstborn has to have everything in exact order and why the lastborn wants to have a party.[1]

This is impacted by differences in gender. We talked earlier about how little girls play together and how their communication centers on relationships. They're focused on what's happening with the group, and their make-believe is about how people relate to each other. You'll hear stories about princesses and personalities and persuasion. If there's conflict, they talk about feelings and attitudes and what's happening in relationships.

Little boys have a competitive wiring that plays out differently. Watch them at play, and they're not talking a lot or sharing their deepest concerns. They're grunting and making truck sounds or imitating the fierce dinosaur. Their "conversation" is about whose truck is bigger, or which dinosaur is stronger. They're not taking turns; they're forcing each other's race cars off the track.

When my oldest granddaughter, Averie, was about eight years old, she was on a softball team. We tried to attend as many of her games as we could and loved watching her play. They had a great coach who was the team's biggest fan, which made the whole thing a positive experience.

When their team was in the field, they were focused on the game. But as soon as they were up to bat, the chain-link dugout was vibrating with conversation. Little clusters of little girls were oblivious to the game because they were busy talking about whatever little girls talk about. Their conversations were animated, and they were focused on each other. When the coach called one of them to bat, a couple of others would scramble to help her find her helmet or bat.

One day, Averie's game was on a field adjoining a boy's game. During a lull in the action, I wandered over to see what was happening there. It was a whole different experience.

In the dugout, the boys weren't standing and talking in groups. They were sitting on the bench, sort of watching the game, waiting until it was their turn to be part of the action. They weren't talking much. Mostly, they were spitting. When they weren't competing on the field, they were competing to see who could spit the farthest.

Maybe it happens, but I've never seen a group of girls having a spitting contest.

If I ask my granddaughters to show me their muscles, they'll flex for me. If I ask five-year-old Marco to show me his muscles, he immediately wants me to do the same so he can compare. And somehow, from his perspective, he can explain how his muscles are bigger than mine.

Since that drive to be the best is hardwired in the brains of boys, they have to figure out what to do with it. So they look to whatever role models they can find to figure it out. If they don't have a dad in the picture (or if that relationship is toxic), they find their role models in television or movies or sports—or each other. When they reach their teen years, they're still trying to figure it out based on what they've observed.

That's why teenage boys often come across as arrogant or brash. Because of that vertical way of relating to others, they try to position themselves as conquerors in most relationships. They find their identity in where they fit in the hierarchy with others. It's not because they're arrogant; it's because they're inexperienced at applying that competitive drive in appropriate ways.

Someday, Marco will be an adult. It wouldn't surprise me if he's having spitting contests with his friends when he's in his thirties. In fact, it wouldn't surprise me if he does the same with his own five-year-old son.

Ok, I admit it: if he challenges me to that contest when I'm in my nineties, I'll do the best I can to beat him.

His Greatest Fears

It's easy to assume that tough guys have no fear. In fact, it's usually part of the description. If someone is the tough hero, it implies that he's not afraid of anything. But there's always an underlying fear that actually drives him to succeed. It's the fear of failure—the fear of *not* making a difference.

That fear is genuine. In the movies, part of the mystique of the hero is his vulnerability. That's what makes him human and draws us to him. He's still the little boy who wants to count for something.

In real life, men don't usually have the opportunity to be an action hero who shows up on the evening news. But the drive is still there to make a difference. So they might take one of two approaches:

1. They become reactive, assuming there's nothing they can do. So they either escape into routine, trying to squash that drive, or lash out in anger.
2. They become proactive, determining to make a difference in the circumstances of their daily life.

The first group might live with a low-grade discouragement, because they feel there's nothing they can do. If a building isn't burning, they can't rescue anyone. So they give up and fill their lives with meaningless entertainment and activities to deaden the pain and ignore the drive that smolders under the surface. It's still there, but they cover it up.

The second group recognizes the reality of their life situation. They want to make a difference, but they're not waiting for opportunity to come to them. They use that drive to find opportunities to impact the lives of others.

It's the difference between glory and giving. The first group operates from a mindset that says, "Look at me! Look at what I can do!" It's the perspective of a little boy who hasn't learned how to capitalize on that drive to be a hero. It's all about how people perceive them. The second group wants to conquer so they can help those in need. It's about making a difference in the lives of others.

True heroes do for others what they can't do for themselves. Most men would rather make an impact in the lives of others than be famous. They might not be leading massive strategies or campaigns in the public eye, but they still want to impact those in their sphere of everyday influence.

What does that mean?

A man wants to make an impact at work, at home, with his family, and with his friends. He wants to be a hero to the real people in his life, the ones who really matter to him.

That includes you—above everyone else.

Why You Matter So Much to Him

The action-film hero will give up everything for the woman he loves. Your man can be wildly successful in his job and in the community. But if he doesn't feel like *your* hero, the rest doesn't matter.

For a number of years, my wife and I worked with a group of young married couples at our church. We were in a mentoring role, spending time with them one-on-one during the week as well as when they came together each Sunday morning.

Often, I would teach the class during those Sunday sessions, which was always a treat. Sometimes, it felt like I had communicated well, my thoughts flowed, and the points were well taken. Other times I felt like I was running through quicksand because I was unsure of what I was saying.

Like most men, I would critique myself mercilessly after each session. I questioned myself the rest of the day about whether or not I had connected with the needs of the group. If I had been comfortable and group members told me my words had been valuable, I felt good. If I had been scattered in my presentation and no one gave me feedback, I felt bad.

I never asked the participants what they thought of the session. I figured that if it was good, they would have said something. If no one approached me, I assumed it wasn't that great.

No matter what other people said, the person I wanted affirmation from the most was my wife. Her perspective mattered more than anyone else's. If she said I did a good job, it gave me everything I needed. Even if she said my thoughts were scattered, that was ok too. I just needed to know that she believed in me and was on my side.

In the car on the way home, I would wait for Diane to give me her thoughts about what I had done. Once in a while she would say, "That was really good today." When that happened, I was on top of the world.

Most of the time she wouldn't say anything. I didn't want to ask, because it felt like I was fishing for compliments. I assumed that if her thoughts were positive she would tell me. So I interpreted her silence as negative. Usually, I would just assume that my talk wasn't that great, and I'd try to mentally set it aside and vow to do better next time.

I finally mentioned to her how I felt when she didn't say anything, and she was shocked. "I figured that you knew it was good, so I didn't need to say anything. When I tell you it's good, it's usually because there's something that spoke directly to me."

We've learned to be more open and honest about our communication since then. But I came to realize that her opinion means more than anyone else's on earth. It was great hearing positive comments from others, but it meant everything to hear them from her. It was her way of saying that I made a difference. It was her way of saying I was her hero.

Men are little boys who want to succeed and are driven to make a difference. But more than that, they want to know that they make a difference to *you*.

Will He Ever Be a Hero?

Let's look at the facts:

- Men have an inner drive to be a hero.
- Most men won't have the opportunity to be a celebrity hero who saves their part of the world.
- They know that, but the drive doesn't go away. So they try to find something they can conquer so they can be a hero at something.

But the quest to become a hero isn't hopeless.

We talked earlier about the action movies that men love so much. Watch them carefully, and you'll probably notice that most of them aren't just about action. The plot usually involves a woman who's important to the hero. The reason he goes to such great lengths to conquer an enemy is to win the heart of that woman.

A man can play video games all day long and strive to reach higher levels of accomplishment. To some degree, it feeds his desire to conquer. In that virtual world, he's making a difference. But he knows it's not making a difference in the real world. If he were making a difference in the real world, he probably wouldn't feel the need to play games as much.

Men who start making a real difference feel the rush of accomplishment, and it can become a driving force. But there's one focal point that energizes him more than any other: making a difference for the woman he cares most about.

In other words, he doesn't just want to be a hero; he wants to be *your* hero.

What does that look like?

As the old saying goes, "A man's home is his castle." Typically, we picture the king going out and conquering the enemy, then coming home and doing the same with his family. He's the hero, so everybody needs to treat him like one. What he really wants is to conquer in the field, then come home to have relationships with the people he cares most about.

The real hero wants to go out and conquer the enemy and make a difference to others. But then he wants to come home and show you what he did. It's not an appeal for fake flattery; it's his need to have his woman recognize that he succeeded in battle—whether financial, physical, corporate, relational, or any other area.

He wants to conquer the world but still be home in time for dinner. It might feel somewhat selfish, but it's real. You won't be able to change it. But if you recognize it, you can capitalize on it. It's actually pretty simple.

Most men don't make the bed because they want the room to look nice. They make the bed because it's a way of being a hero, meeting the needs of their woman. Express simple gratefulness and he'll feel respected—and inclined to do it more often. Criticize his performance because the pillows are crooked and he'll feel discouraged.

Your man sees himself through your eyes. You can't force him to behave in a certain way. But if you see him through eyes of respect, he'll see himself as your hero. If he believes that, you'll be meeting the basic need he has for your respect. Over time, he'll be inclined to get off the couch and do anything for you.

Men are wired to make a difference.

They want to make a difference with you.

PART 3

How He Acts

Central Park in New York doesn't have a great reputation. I'd heard about it for years and seen it on television and in the movies. It's a background for crime dramas and sinister scenes in scary films. National news reports describe murders and attacks that take place there. I always pictured it as a place where you couldn't walk without your life being in danger.

Earlier this week, I was in New York for a speaking engagement and staying about three blocks from Central Park. I decided to go to the park for a run one evening. I went online to see what people were saying about it in terms of safety. Most of what I read said that there were some areas of the park that were questionable, but mostly at night and off the main roads.

So I was a little nervous, even though it was still daylight outside. I entered the park cautiously, looking around constantly to make sure I wasn't going to get in trouble.

That's when I realized I wasn't alone. In the time I was there, I probably saw five hundred other runners. Horse-drawn carriages took other people on tours, and hundreds more people walked or played on the green, rolling hills and rock formations. It was incredible and amazing, one of those experiences I'll never forget.

And I almost missed it because I had accepted an incomplete perspective.

That happens in relationships with men too. There are a ton of stereotypes the media has portrayed about men that are incomplete or untrue. "Men don't have feelings" or "men don't listen" are just a couple of the generalizations that many people have come to accept as true.

But that perspective can keep women from experiencing the best that a man has to offer. We need to expose those stereotypes and challenge them. We can learn what's accurate about men and what comes from urban legends. We can find out why men really act the way they do, and what it really means.

6

Why He Can't See Dirt

Men do things that irritate women.

I know that might come as a surprise, but it's true. Irritating things usually show up after a relationship has been going for a while, not at the beginning.

When a relationship starts, you're attracted by the good things. The irritating things are there, but you haven't noticed them yet. "Love is blind" becomes a reality as you're enamored of the man's charms and wit and looks and humor. It takes time for the irritations to start showing up.

The first time he burps in public, it catches your attention. You assume it was an accident, because you know he wouldn't have done it on purpose. It does seem a little strange, though, that he didn't say "Excuse me." It's not until a few months later, when he wins a burping contest with friends, that celibacy begins to sound attractive.

I recently asked some female co-workers what irritated them most about men. They were quick to respond.

"I ask for his opinion about something, and he just says, 'I don't care.'"

"He falls asleep on the couch watching television, but wakes up when I change the channel and says, 'Hey! I was watching that!'"

"I just finish cleaning the kitchen and he comes in and messes it up."

"When we go someplace, he always wants me to put his stuff in my purse so he doesn't have to carry it."

"He doesn't notice when I get a new haircut—or if he does, he doesn't compliment me. He just says, 'You changed your hair.'"

"He talks on his phone when we're out to dinner."

"He leaves the toilet seat up. Doesn't he know what that means for a woman when she gets up in the night?"

"He wants to take me out but wants me to plan it."

"He can't see dirt."

Let's take that last one. Is it true that men can't see dirt? I reviewed a number of different sources to see if there had been any research on it. I couldn't find anything except blog posts and humor articles describing the phenomenon.

I think there's a different question: When women see "dirt," exactly what are they looking at?

Men think of dirt as a clump of mud on the carpet, black smudges on the countertop, or spaghetti sauce that jumped onto their shirt. It's something obvious. Anything more subtle doesn't qualify as "dirt" in their mind.

So when a woman says, "The kitchen is filthy," she might mean that it's been a long time since it's been scrubbed.

It often reflects the fact that since food is prepared in the kitchen, it feels unsanitary if the counters haven't been wiped down with something that kills germs. It's not obvious grime as much as just knowing there's a thin layer of something that needs to be removed.

A man walks into a kitchen that has been described as filthy and wonders what the problem is. He doesn't see clumps of mud, black smudges, or pools of spaghetti sauce. If she asks him to clean the kitchen, he won't know where to start, what to do, or how to know when it's done.

Several years ago, my wife and I discussed the issue of chores around the house. Since I work out of a home office, I'm around on the days when I'm not traveling or leading seminars. Diane is self-employed, but works with clients outside the home. So we're both in and out during the day. In general, I normally handle repairs and she handles the bulk of the cleaning. We both mow the lawn and water plants and do other chores, and if one of us washes our own car, we'll typically wash the other's car as well.

For the regular household chores, we agreed that I would be responsible for scrubbing the toilets weekly, cleaning our guest bathroom each week, vacuuming twice a week, and collecting the trash the day before pickup. Those are actually chores I don't mind much, because I get a sense of satisfaction when I polish things, and if I complete those things then Diane feels like I'm contributing fairly to the chores.

When I started doing these chores, I discovered that Diane and I had a different idea of what "clean" looked like. She didn't want to come in and clean after me, because it would imply that I wasn't doing a good job, and I really did want her to be pleased with my work (I wanted to be the hero). So I asked her to show me what clean looked like when she did it.

I watched her clean our guest bathroom step-by-step. From my perspective, she was cleaning things that weren't dirty. She cleaned mirrors that didn't have spots, wiped counters that had no visible impurities, and cleaned floors that didn't show any grime. When she was done, it didn't look any different to me than it did before she started.

Today, I clean the bathroom exactly the way that's important to her. I don't see the dirt, but I don't care. It's important to her, so I do it her way out of respect for her.

Vacuuming is the same thing. I know dirt gets on the floor, but I don't see it. I'm guessing it's really dust, not dirt. But Diane knows it's there and that it needs to be removed if the house is going to be clean. When I vacuum, I'm not doing it to remove dirt. I'm doing it to make symmetrical lines in the carpet so it looks clean. I've often thought I could take a stick and draw symmetrical lines and accomplish the same thing.

After months of vacuuming, Diane decided it was time to clean the carpet. Again, I didn't see any dirt, but she was convinced that our grandkids would develop some lifelong disease if they played on it. So I rented a self-service carpet cleaner, followed the instructions, filled it with hot, soapy water, and did a few passes across the carpet until it was time to empty the holding tank.

When I did, the water was black. Not light gray, not medium gray. Black. I realized Diane had been right. I couldn't see the dirt, but it was there. I don't know if she could actually see it, but she sensed it. Guys don't do that.

I could give multiple examples of things men do that irritate women. But they usually don't do them intentionally.

Women are frustrated that men can't see dirt, and men are frustrated because they can't see the dirt their woman sees. It just reinforces the fact that men and women see things differently.

It's not a matter of who's right and who's wrong, which is a conversation that's doomed from the start. It's recognizing and valuing the true differences in each other.

Simple Simon

Because of how their brains work, men aren't that complicated. Women's brains tend to connect everything with everything else, while men tend to focus on one thing at a time. So when men do things that are irritating, they're not trying to irritate you. They're just being men.

Case in point: recently, I was wearing a pair of slacks and evidently sat in something oily that left a small stain. It was close to the inseam on one leg, near the back of my pants. It didn't come out in the wash, so Diane said that I needed to get rid of them.

She was thinking about the fact that I would be in a professional setting, standing in front of groups, and have a stain on my pants. I was thinking that it wasn't a problem because it was in a place where no one would ever see it. We talked about it, and it was helpful to hear her reasoning and to express my perspective. I ended up keeping the pants, but she's ok because we talked it through. I know it still bothers her, but she decided it wasn't a battle worth fighting.

And no one has ever seen the stain. I don't think.

Instead of becoming frustrated with each other because we think the other person is crazy, Diane and I have learned to explore each other's positions. That's become a key for us. Sometimes one of us will defer to the other because the "battle" isn't that important. Other times we'll simply live with the differences—not because we understand but because we appreciate the reality of those differences. We care more about our relationship than who's right.

So when my favorite black pullover sweater got a major hole in the armpit, she was going to throw it out. "You're constantly raising your arms when you're talking, so it'll be obvious," she said. "You can't wear that." My first response was, "I'll wear a black T-shirt under it, and nobody will know the difference." I was serious, and so was she.

Her position made more sense than mine, so I let that one go. Again, sometimes you have to pick your battles.

It Goes Both Ways

Men have similar questions about women, but often don't think to ask.

- They wonder how you're able to see dirt that they don't.
- They want to know why you make the bed every morning when you're just going to get back in that evening.
- They have no idea what to say when you ask them, "Does this make me look fat?"
- They want to know why you go to the restroom in groups when dining out.
- They want to know why your description of a situation sometimes takes longer than the actual situation did.

Here's a common example that's the reverse of the dirt question. Men wonder, *Why can't women see the importance of sports on television?* Many women love sports, but it's much more prevalent with men. Men often enjoy sports because it fits with their need to conquer and win. They don't spend a lot of time analyzing that need; they just enjoy it and find themselves drawn to it.

So when they're in the middle of watching a game, they aren't paying much attention to anything else. Their male brain has chosen that one thing to focus on, so everything else diminishes during that time. When a woman asks a man a question during a game, he might not hear it. His brain is focused on what's happening in the game, so the question is almost like a familiar voice coming from outside. It doesn't quite register. The woman gets frustrated because he's more interested in the game than in her, and it increases her frustration with his game-watching habit. Meanwhile, he's confused because he doesn't know what he did wrong.

Dealing with the Differences

It goes back to the bottom line: it's not a matter of who's right or wrong; it's recognizing that we're different. When a woman feels frustrated with a man because of his actions, she usually responds in one of three ways:

1. She tries to change him.
2. She keeps it inside.
3. She talks to him about it.

Let's explore each of those options.

1. She tries to change him.

This one is probably the most ineffective response and sets the relationship up for even more conflict. It's based on the assumption that the man's behavior is *wrong* instead of *different*, and needs to be fixed.

I read a lot of articles and books about this topic when I was writing *People Can't Drive You Crazy If You Don't Give Them the Keys.*[1] I found lengthy discussions about the reasons people do what they do and different approaches to dealing with frustration in relationships. But it always boiled down to one question: Can I change another person?

The answer is a simple one, and true in most cases: no.

Think about how hard it is to change ourselves. We commit to losing weight but give up when a chocolate chip cookie crosses our path. We promise ourselves we'll have a better attitude until someone else's crummy attitude affects us. We decide to read more but have trouble turning off the television. We have great intentions, but those habits and patterns have been in place for a really long time. Even when our desire is strong, changing ourselves usually feels like a losing battle.

We're not alone. With a few exceptions, everybody is pretty much who they were five years ago. If we can't change ourselves, how futile is it to think we can change someone else? In fact, think of how we feel when someone tries to change us. In most cases we resist, because it feels like they're saying we're not good enough the way we are. It implies that until we change, they're not satisfied with us.

Real relationships happen when two people accept each other as they are, including their differences. When that happens, they feel safe in the relationship. When they feel safe, they're often motivated to change. They know they'll still be accepted the way they are, whether they change or not. They're valued for who they are, not who they aren't.

That doesn't mean you have to excuse a man's poor behavior. It means discerning between behavior and wiring, recognizing whether something comes from his male brain or from his choices. If it's from his maleness, it's part of who he is. Trying to change it will lead to frustration. If it comes from his choices, you still can't force him to change—but you can influence him.

2. She keeps it inside.

This response is more than just ineffective; it's toxic. It starts with low-grade irritation but turns into industrial-strength bitterness over time. When we don't deal with the issue, we never "get over it." It gets stuck inside, growing and festering until our attitude toward the other person becomes more and more negative. We try to act like nothing is wrong, but it's building on the inside.

When a crisis happens, it all explodes at once. We feel better, but everyone else is wondering, "What was that all about?" and there's a big mess to clean up.

It's like shaking a can of soda. Pressure builds in the can, but no one sees it. There are protective walls that keep everything inside. But pop the top and soda will spray everywhere.

We've all had situations where we had a strong emotion (such as anger) building up for days or even weeks. We don't tell anyone about it, and it swells inside. If conversations do happen, they're often lightly laced with sarcasm, hinting at the pressure that's behind the words. If we choose to have a genuine heart-to-heart conversation about it, that would release the pressure. Just talking to another person about what we're feeling is often enough to release the power it has over us.

Someone said, "In the absence of facts, we tend to make up data to support our beliefs." That's true when it comes to men and women. You get frustrated with a partner because of something he does but you don't talk about it. You interpret his motives through a female perspective when his motives might be totally different. He probably isn't trying to ruin your life. In fact, he probably doesn't even realize what he's doing.

Whenever we assume what another person is thinking or feeling, we're usually wrong. It's that simple. We're not them, and we don't have their brain, so we can't see what's going on inside that brain unless we ask.

That leads to the third approach.

3. She talks to him about it.

This response is the only healthy one and is only possible when she accepts the reality of the differences in how men think. It means having an "exploring" conversation rather than an "accusing" one. It's a conversation that needs to take place early, before assumptions start to build up.

Emotions can become the trigger for recognizing the need for this conversation, signaling to us that something in the relationship needs attention. When a woman can't understand why a man does something, it's appropriate to approach him to explore.

"But he gets frustrated when I try to talk to him about this stuff," you say. "He feels like I'm picking on him."

That's why the approach is so critical. If it comes across as accusatory, he'll automatically be on the defensive. If it comes off as exploratory, it's seen as a sign of respect and affirmation.

Listen to the difference in how these two sentences come across to a man.

> "You're always looking at your phone when I'm try-
> ing to talk to you. You care more about that stupid
> phone than about me." (Accusatory)

With that approach, a man feels like he's done something wrong and is in trouble. It makes him defensive instead of open to what you're saying.

> "I need your help in figuring something out." (Wait for
> response.) "I've noticed that a lot of times, when
> I come to talk to you, you're looking at something
> on your phone. I'm not sure how to handle that, be-
> cause it feels like you're distracted or like you're not
> that interested in what I'm saying. Am I reading it
> wrong?" (Exploratory)

In that second approach, you're more likely to get the response you're after. It's not guaranteed, but you've opened the conversation with respect, making it about what you're feeling instead of what he's doing. He might not give you the answer you're looking for, saying something like, "I'm just good at multitasking." That response probably isn't accurate, but you've opened the door for future conversations. You treated him with respect, and you did it before emotions escalated. It's a conversation you can revisit later as an open dialogue.

Winning with Influence

We can't change other people. We can only change ourselves. By changing the way we approach things, we influence others and keep our communication channels open. When that happens, they might choose to change.

The key for women dealing with the differences in men is threefold:

1. Recognize the reality of those differences.
2. See them as different, not wrong.
3. Make choices in how to respond to those differences in a way that values the relationship.

When men feel that a woman accepts their male differences without trying to change them, it gives them the safety to change themselves because they want to please that woman.

If your man learns your definition of dirt, he might even begin to see it.

7

Your Knight in Rusting Armor

hate Richard Gere.

Not really. I enjoy watching his movies. But he makes it tough for us guys, because he knows how to be romantic onscreen. He's handsome, charming, and says all the right things at the right time in the right way with the right tone of voice. He's the strong, silent type who shows control and knows how to sweep women off their feet with a glance and a smile.

He makes me feel like a loser in the romance department.

My wife and I watched one of his movies in the theater a few years ago called *Shall We Dance?* Gere takes ballroom dance lessons behind his wife's back so he can surprise her. The movie is great because the focus is on how much he loves his wife and the lengths he will go to in order to please her. In other words, he was taking romance lessons.

The pivotal scene takes place in a deserted department store. His wife has been suspicious that he's been having an affair during those times he's been gone taking lessons, when suddenly he appears. His wife is stunned as she watches him rise to the top of the escalator in a black tuxedo, red bow tie, and a single rose for her.

I heard my wife catch her breath. I thought she was going to pass out in the seat next to me. I watched the scene and her response and thought, *Ok, I'd love to be that romantic. But it's just not me. I'll never measure up.*

That's the point: men will never measure up to the scripted, fairy-tale view of romance that comes across on the big screen. All that men know about romance is what they see and hear, and it seems out of reach. That doesn't mean we can't romance our woman in a way that takes her breath away. We shouldn't just give up.

Women want to be romanced. That's why romance novels are so popular—they give women a chance to experience it vicariously through fictional characters. The top ten most popular topics on the Romance Writers of America website, in the order of popularity, are:

1. Friends to lovers
2. Soul mates/fate
3. Second chance at love
4. Secret romance
5. First love
6. Strong hero/heroine
7. Reunited lovers
8. Love triangle

9. Sexy billionaire/millionaire
10. Sassy heroine

It's also revealing that 84 percent of readers of these books are women between the ages of thirty and fifty-four. Someone suggested that in their twenties, women are still hoping their man will change and become more romantic. But by the time they turn thirty, women have given up and turn to novels instead.

The Flip Side

At the same time, most men *want* to be romantic. But if they believe they have to write poetry and dance elegantly and say just the right things all the time, they'll give up before they start. When they hold themselves to that standard, they feel inferior. It feels artificial, and they're not very good actors. In a sense, they're too honest to pretend to be something they're not.

The reason? Most men are still little boys who want to be heroes. But if it involves romantic behavior, the risk is too great. He's afraid he'll be laughed at or criticized for not "doing it right." He has an unrealistic perspective of what romance is, and no one has told him otherwise.

Somebody needs to show him that romance comes from who he is, and you're the best person to help him discover what that looks like. It's the intentional use of his uniqueness that captures a woman's heart. That's what she falls in love with. He doesn't know that, and will never find out unless he hears it from you.

I recently had a conversation with a man about his relationship with his wife. I said, "So, what's the one thing you wish your wife understood most about you?" His response was simple. "I just wish she knew how deeply I love her. I just don't know how to express it."

I've heard that over and over again from men. They have this deep emotional attachment to that most important woman in their life, but they feel inadequate at being romantic. It's like those emotions get stuck inside, and they get frustrated when their woman tells them they're not romantic enough. They really want to be, but don't know how.

So, What Does Romance Look Like?

I wanted to find out how women defined romance. I did some research and then asked several female friends for their perspective. Here are some of the things I heard:

"I don't care what he does, as long as it shows that he loves me."

"I want him to remind me that he's in this for the long haul—that he's sticking with me no matter what."

"He accepts me just the way I am."

"He understands the 'for better or worse' stuff, because I'm not always the most lovable. But he hangs in there with me."

"He surprises me with a text in the middle of the day, letting me know that he's thinking of me."

"When he's on a business trip and sees a beautiful sunset, he takes a picture of it and sends it with a text that says, 'Wish you were here with me to see this.'"

"He holds my hand when we're shopping."

"He tells me what's going on in his life that concerns him."

"He drew a little heart on the bathroom mirror with my lipstick so I'd find it later in the day."

"He vacuums. By choice."

"He simply holds me for a few extra seconds."

Two things surprised me about that list:

1. There was no mention of chocolate, jewelry, or ascending an escalator in a tuxedo.
2. They were all things I, as a man, would feel comfortable doing.

That doesn't mean women don't appreciate gifts that are a true expression of what their man is feeling. But for the most part, a woman's view of romance seems to revolve around a man being intentional while being himself. It means putting his woman in the center of his radar and finding natural ways to let her know that she's there.

The best definition of romance I heard was from an anonymous source: "You don't love someone for their looks, or their clothes, or their fancy car, but because they sing a song only you can hear." A man might not be able to carry a tune, but *his* heart sings a song that can carry *your* heart. If he doesn't get to express it, he starts to forget the words and the melody.

I've always wanted to write a song for Diane. I thought it would be great if I could put into words what I felt about her and then find someone to wrap music around those words.

But I don't write songs. If that's my standard of romance, I'm doomed.

Other people have written some really great words that I would like to have said. I've realized that even though I might not be able to write the song myself, I can download it and give it to her as a gift. "If I could write you a song," I've told her, "this would be what it would say."

I have found other creative ways to use other people's expressions as my own. For example, greeting cards can be expensive. I'll usually buy my wife one for her birthday or our anniversary. I used to feel obligated to buy the cards, or flowers, or other traditional sentiments. After all, that's what all the advertising says that women want. But it never felt like I was being genuine about romance, even though I wanted to be.

We talked about it once, and she helped me understand her perspective. It wasn't the purchases that made it special, but the fact that I was thinking about her and being intentional about showing my love for her. I didn't realize that until she told me, and her affirmation helped me learn how to be romantic without the pressure. I could be myself.

Now, on most special days (or just random trips to the store), we'll spend a few minutes in the card section, looking for the perfect card to express our love for each other. Once we've found the right ones, we show them to each other, kiss, and put them back. We get the impact in a way that is fun and meaningful for both of us.

Romantic? I don't expect anyone to make a movie based on it. But it's a small, intentional expression of what I feel for my wife. It's something I can do that fits my temperament, and she's ok with it. It fits her style too.

How come nobody ever told us this stuff? If they had, we might be a whole lot better at this romance thing.

Fanning the Flame

So, if most men are romantically impaired because of unrealistic standards, what can be done? It's not foolproof, but it's simple: you have to tell him what romance is to *you* in a way that he'll believe.

The greatest need a man has from a woman is to be respected. In fact, several studies found a man's need for respect is greater than his need for love or sex. If a man doesn't feel that she respects him, he'll starve emotionally.[1] Not knowing how to handle that, he gets frustrated because his needs aren't being met. That might come out as anger, which the woman can't understand because she's trying to show him love and it's not working.

Remember our previous discussion about the struggle men have with insecurity, and how they do everything they can to avoid it? They have a natural drive to succeed and show competence in every area of their life, and feel like less of a person when that doesn't happen.

If a man is doing well at work, his boss acknowledges it and pays him for his performance. If he is a respected leader in his church or community, he feels accomplished and hears that he's making a difference. But if he doesn't feel like he's competent at home as a husband, lover, and friend because you don't tell him, it sends him back to insecurity.

Men need to hear affirmation from their favorite woman. That meets their need for respect and personal security. No matter what recognition he receives on the job or in the community, it means nothing if he doesn't have an affirmation of respect from his wife.

Ken Blanchard, author of *The One Minute Manager*, talks about the importance of "catching people doing something right."[2] He says that many employees only hear from their bosses when they do something wrong. It's sometimes called "Seagull Management"—where the boss occasionally swoops in, dumps, and disappears, leaving everyone in a mess. Ken suggests that a single, intentional word of encouragement can make all the difference in how an employee feels. When they're encouraged, they feel confident. When they feel confident, they want to repeat the behavior.

The same thing is true of men. Affirm them for something they've done that's positive, and they'll go out of their way to do it in the future. Why? Because it felt so good to have your affirmation.

In a sense, they become who you see them to be.

Style has never been one of my strong points. I don't have a lot of security in the patterns and colors I put together. But once in a while, I go somewhere with a shirt and tie that evidently go well together. I've had women I didn't even know compliment me on the combination, and I found myself wearing those clothes almost daily after that.

I was going through a TSA checkpoint at the airport a few weeks ago and a female agent said, "That color goes great with your eyes." Guess what shirt I wear now when I want to feel confident? It means even more when that affirmation comes from my wife, because I know it's coming from a place of respect. (If men respond to the positive comments of a TSA officer, think how much more they'll be impacted by their woman's affirmation.)

Of course, respect is so much more than affirming men in their clothing choices. You can have a huge influence by catching your man doing things right—romantically. Keep your eyes and ears open for little things he does that make you feel loved, and let him know. Say, "You know, you swept off the deck yesterday. That's something I usually do, but that was really special that you did that. I know it sounds strange, but you doing that made me feel loved and closer to you. Thanks."

From a man's perspective, I can tell you that he'll probably be sweeping the deck almost daily after that, because you met his deep need to feel respected. He'll probably start looking for other things he can do to get a similar response from you in the future.

Give him permission to not be Richard Gere. Give him permission to be himself.

Opportunities to Influence Romance

When you let your man know what real romance looks like to you, you free him to explore options that fit his personality and temperament. Don't expect overnight results, because those patterns have been reinforced by society and the media for a long time. It's not automatic, and it's not guaranteed. It's just the quickest way to meet his hardwired drive to matter to you.

It's not that complicated, because men aren't that complicated. He wants to feel the respect and admiration of the most important woman in his life. When that happens, he'll feel like a hero, which means he'll be more inclined to do heroic things.

When a relationship begins, most men go overboard to be romantic. It seems like you're the whole focus of his attention. He brings you flowers, talks to you for hours on end, and goes without sleep just to spend more time with you. From a woman's perspective, it makes sense to assume that he'll always be that way. After all, it's part of who he is, right? That's why he does those things. But over time, that flame starts to dim and changes into a warm glow instead of burning brightly. If left unattended, the fire could go out.

When my daughter's husband was first dating her in high school, he wanted to ask her to the prom. She was living at home, so he asked us for permission to come to our house while she was away so he could set up his invitation. I don't remember all it consisted of, but it involved a detailed sign in her closet, lots of decorations, and a lengthy trail of Hershey's kisses throughout the house that led her to her destination.

She was impressed, and she said yes. They went to the prom together. A few years later, they were married. Now, after fifteen-plus years and three kids, things look a little different. I reminded him over lunch a few months ago about that event, and asked him if he had showered her with chocolate kisses lately. He chuckled and said, "Well, probably not. Plus, the dog or the kids would get them before she would find them." He loves his wife deeply, but their relationship looks different than it did in high school.

It might seem like a man isn't being honest because he starts by being so romantic and then quits. But it goes back to the way his brain is wired. Men are wired for conquering, competing, and winning. He's not trying to be selfish, but he's attracted to a woman and wants to win her heart. At that stage, it's a great quest that challenges his abilities. He'll do whatever he can to gain her commitment to a relationship. He's focused and determined. He wants to win, in the best sense of the word.

The problem is that most men are better at conquering than they are at maintaining. Once they've won a woman's heart, they've achieved their objective. Inside their brain, they've accomplished their mission and it's time for the next challenge. That doesn't mean he loves her any less; it means that he won't naturally be as focused on courting as he was before.

If that's true, a woman shouldn't be surprised if her man changes his behavior after she says yes. She should recognize that he deeply cares for her but has moved on to a new season in the relationship. He's leaving the conquering season behind and replacing it with a building season.

On the other hand, it doesn't mean she has to give up on him improving. Maintaining a relationship is out of his comfort zone, and he hasn't had much practice. In most cases, he really wants to be a good partner and give his woman what she needs. Since it's new, it will take intentional effort.

That means he'll make mistakes. If you focus on his mistakes, he'll get discouraged. If you focus on his efforts to learn and do it right, he'll be encouraged to improve.

You think it's romantic if he goes shopping with you. He hates shopping. You've let him know how much it would mean to you, so he goes along. If he's grumpy, it's easy to get frustrated. Instead, just say, "I know this is pretty low on your list of 'favorite' things to do. I know you're not having a good time. We'll keep it short—but I want you to know how much it means to me that you came along. It feels romantic to me because it tells me you care enough to come."

It probably won't make him any less grumpy at the moment, but your words will stick. A few weeks later, he invites you to go shopping with him, but takes you to Home Depot. You might feel like saying, "Nice try, but wrong place. This isn't romantic at all."

But look through his eyes. He's attempting to do what you asked, which was to go shopping. Going to Home Depot is special to him, and he thinks of it as a chance to spend time with you doing something he enjoys. Acknowledge the effort and enjoy the journey.

Diane has picked up on my attraction to Home Depot. Whenever we go there together, it's a special event. I always open the car door for her, and we hold hands as we walk through the store. I'm in my favorite store with my favorite woman.

It doesn't get much better than that.

The key to this whole romance thing is communication. A man can't read a woman's mind, and she can't read his. When we make assumptions about another person's motives without asking them, it almost always leads to frustration. The only way to find out what another person is thinking is to ask them, and do it in a safe environment.

What does "safe" mean? When a woman asks a man to tell her what he's thinking, it's risky for him. He'll probably take that risk, but her response will determine how much he risks in the future.

If she gets defensive, argues, or tries to explain her position when he shares his feelings, it's not safe. He'll shut down because she wasn't really listening. But if she listens for understanding instead of agreement, asking questions instead of telling her perspective, it's safe. He learns that he can trust her with his feelings because she protects them.

In that kind of environment, communication grows. When communication grows, relationships grow. Honest communication isn't always easy, and there will always be things that are uncomfortable or messy.

That's ok. Messy, honest, safe communication becomes fertile soil for romance to grow.

Your man might turn out to be more romantic than you ever imagined.

8

Unconditional Like

This chapter begins with a disclaimer.

After I finished writing it, my wife read through it. She said, "If I didn't know you, I'd feel like you were telling me that I had to do all the changing in my relationship with my man. Your female readers are going to think, 'How come I have to change? What about him? It sounds like it's all my responsibility and he's off the hook!'"

That's not my intention at all. It's not women's fault, and men absolutely have things they need to work on in any relationship.

But this book isn't a marriage or relationship manual about how to change another person. It's an *understanding* manual. We're exploring what happens in a man's mind and how it impacts the choices he makes every day. My goal is to walk with you and show you the sights. Once you see that perspective clearly, you'll be able to make unique, customized decisions about how to handle the man in your life.

So keep that in mind as you read. If something feels unfair or one-sided, remember, I'm not letting the man off the hook. I'm just trying to help you understand him accurately.

There are a lot of stereotypes about men:

- They won't listen to women.
- They're not emotional.
- They're threatened by independent women.
- All they think about is sex.
- They'll cheat if they're given the chance.
- They're afraid of commitment.
- They'd rather hang out with their guy friends.

Where do those stereotypes come from? Are they true?

When women get together, they might talk about the men in their lives. They might be frustrated by something their man has done, and they're trying to figure out his motives. If they believe those stereotypes they'll say things like:

"Well, he's a man—so what do you expect?"

"He's just not capable of doing that; it's just the way men are."

"Men—can't live with them, can't live without them."

How should a woman respond to these perspectives? She should challenge those stereotypes to see if they're true for her man by exploring other perspectives with him. Women and men both want real relationships, not ones where they have to "perform" in a certain way. Real relationships happen when a woman engages with her man to explore who he really is, how he's unique, and how he really thinks.

Let's explore how that works.

Breaking Down the Walls

Guys don't like to be stereotyped by women, but most of them have heard it their entire lives. Sure, there are some guys who use those stereotypes as an excuse: "I'm a guy—it's just how I am." But deep inside, they know those things aren't true; they just don't know what to say to counter them. So they don't say anything.

It starts on the playground, where most guys are taught to hide their emotions.

Kai is only eight years old but knows how it feels if someone calls him a sissy. If he shows any emotion, his friends (or even his dad) will pounce on him and tell him to "act like a man." He's trying to figure out what manhood looks like by watching other boys and how they react to things. So he suppresses his natural sensitivity so he'll be perceived as "a man."

We end up with boys who won't show their vulnerability and grow into men who won't show their vulnerability. That's unfortunate, because vulnerability is exactly what connects with women. It's in there, tucked away but not expressed. When women don't see any emotions, they generalize that men just aren't that emotional.

It's time to test those stereotypes to see if they're true. How? By having a safe conversation with your man about them.

In this setting, "safe" means exploring some of the stereo-types with him but not reacting in ways that reinforce them. If a woman overreacts or becomes critical when a man starts to test the waters of vulnerability, he'll step back on shore and be hesitant to try again.

He might become suspicious when you begin exploring. But deep inside, he wants you to know the truth about him. When a man has the chance to express his needs accurately with his woman, it frees him to do something he's rarely done in the past. If you're the safe person he does that with, it builds trust and bonds him to you in your relationship.

So, you've heard the stereotypes. What do men *really* want you to know?

The Top Fourteen Needs of Men

Through research and conversations with men over the years, I've found certain themes repeated consistently. They all have to do with breaking those stereotypes and letting women see what's really going on inside. Here are the things I heard the most often that men want women to know—from their perspective.

1. We want you to communicate directly.

We really want to know what you're thinking. Sometimes we get impatient because you take a long time to describe a situation. Sure, we'd like you to get to the point faster. But that doesn't mean we don't care. The process just gets in the way.

We can't read your mind, so the only way we'll know what you want is if you tell us. Don't try to manipulate us into doing something out of guilt; just tell us straight up what you want. Tell us the truth, as simply as you can. Don't assume we don't care. Assume we do, and give us a chance to explore that with you.

2. We love your emotions when you express them well.

We don't want you to suppress your emotions or hide them from us. How you handle your emotions is huge for us. We love your emotions and want to see them—when they're not out of control. Anger, sadness, and strong emotions are part of who you are, and we want to be with you when you're feeling them. It's just that we don't know what to do when you explode.

That doesn't mean you can't have strong emotions and express them. It means we respond better if you've learned how to express your emotions appropriately in a way that doesn't attack us. Men respect women who have a healthy use of their emotional power.

3. We want you to be independent.

Someone said, "Two half-people don't make one whole relationship." We need to become a healthy, whole person, and we need you to as well. We want you to need us but not be dependent on us.

Contrary to what a lot of people think, most men don't want to be in a relationship with a weak person so that they can feel stronger. There are some controlling men who feel that way, but we're talking about healthy men. That perspective isn't healthy. Secure women inspire us. Don't give up your interests to be with us, but when you are with us, give us 100 percent.

It's impressive to us when you have your own life outside of us. It tells us that you've chosen us to be partners in this process of life, and we're both bringing our own health and wholeness into the relationship.

Simply stated, we need you to like yourself. When you do, it's easy and natural for us to give you our respect.

4. Treat us with kindness.

A lot of women are afraid to tell their man their honest feelings because they're afraid of how he will respond. It's well deserved in a lot of cases because men can be pretty insensitive. When they haven't had a lot of practice using emotions, they default to one that's acceptable for a man, like anger (which often comes across as sarcasm or withdrawal).

No matter how we respond, we're still human. Humans tend to respond to others in the way they're approached. If someone approaches us with kindness, it's easier to respond in the same way. When they approach us with sarcasm, it's natural to use sarcasm in response. That's why King Solomon said, "A gentle answer turns away wrath."[1]

Men and women in a relationship care about each other. That's why they got together in the first place. If they care that much and see enough value in each other that they're together, wouldn't it make sense to treat each other with kindness and respect?

The more value something has, the more we treat it with care. We handle an expensive crystal goblet differently than we do a plastic sippy cup. No matter what men say, it builds trust when you make kindness your default setting.

5. We respond to praise.

Some women feel like it's wrong to praise their husband because it might reinforce bad behavior. When a woman is frustrated, she might not see the good as much as she sees the bad. In her frustration, her conversation centers around things her man is doing wrong instead of focusing on what he's doing right.

Praise (when it's genuine) is the fuel that helps us move forward. If we only hear criticism, it makes us critical. But when men hear praise, it builds our confidence. Most important, the praise we get from you means more than all the praise we get elsewhere combined.

It doesn't have to be big. Just let us know when you catch us doing something right. It will make us want to do it even more.

It's especially powerful when you're honestly frustrated with us (and we know it) but still praise us for something positive we did in the middle of it. "I'm really irritated with you right now over this whole situation," you say. "But when we were talking about my sister's meddling in our lives, you listened to me. You didn't try to fix it or figure it out; you just listened. I felt like you heard me. That was good. I really appreciate that. Ok, now about our situation . . ." That kind of response is powerful because it's unexpected, and you wouldn't have said it in that setting if it wasn't genuine.

Our brains are wired for honest praise. Don't overlook that.

6. We don't want to cheat on you.

That's a big one, because a lot of women feel like a man will cheat if he has the opportunity. Because of how we're wired, other women catch our eye even if we're satisfied. If we've chosen to be in a relationship with you, it's because we want you to be the one who satisfies us. We're probably more vulnerable when things are rocky in our relationship, but if the relationship is healthy, we won't stray. We know we'll grow by working through it.

A good man has a keen desire for fidelity. He values it and will work hard to stay faithful to his woman. At the same time, it's important that you don't cheat on him, either. We want the trust that comes from mutual commitment to each other. We really do—that's why we entered into a committed relationship with you. If we're dating, we set ourselves apart from others to give our attention to our relationship. If we're married, we want it to be a lifelong commitment.

That doesn't mean men never stray. It happens more often than we'd like to admit. But know that it's not our intent. A good man doesn't want to cheat and will take every precaution to keep it from happening. When that commitment is mutual, it builds the kind of trust that can weather the storms of a relationship.

7. We want you to be playful.

Nobody gets into a relationship because they want to be bored. Most men have grown up with a bias for activity. They like doing things more than talking. They were brought up on play, so it's part of who they are. So when a woman is playful, she's found the secret door to his heart.

Men are more attracted by the experiences a woman creates with them than the things she says. To capture the imagination of a man, a woman who "does" has more leverage than a woman who "says." Men want to have fun, and they would like to do it with you. If they enter a relationship with a woman and she's not playful, it's not fun anymore. When that relationship becomes tedious, it won't be the source of energy for him that it normally would be.

Playfulness doesn't just mean doing events together. It's an overall attitude of fun and enjoyment that permeates the whole relationship. When you're enjoying the relationship, it gives a man what he needs to enjoy it himself.

Women tend to be more responsible and organized. They plan their weeks and their days and set a path for each day. When they're working on one thing, they're mentally transitioning to the three things they'll be doing when that one is done.

A man tends to be much more spontaneous (maybe *impulsive* is a better word). When he feels like going out for dinner, it takes a woman off guard: "But I already thawed out the leftover meatloaf. Let's go some other time." It doesn't have to happen every time, but it means a lot to a man if occasionally you say, "Well, I was planning on having leftovers, and I just thawed them out. But it would be a nice break to go out. Let's do it, and we can have the leftovers tomorrow night."

For a man, that's fun. When he knows a woman has made plans, it means a lot to him that she will let them go to be spontaneous with him. It tells him that he's more important to her than the meatloaf. That keeps him energized in the relationship.

8. We need passion.

It's true that men have a strong need for sexual fulfillment in an appropriate relationship. It's more than a desire; it's a need. Passion is something different. Passion, to a man, says that you have a strong emotional sense of attraction to him. He wants to be desired. In fact, several studies found that men have more fear of being in a relationship where there's no passion or attraction than they have fear of commitment.

We might know that you love us. But we need you to like us too. Sure, there will be challenging times where we're both irritated. But relationships start because of attraction and continue because of attraction. That's what passion looks like to a man, and it's the fuel that keeps him focused on you. It can't be faked, because men can spot that easily. You can be creative as to how it's expressed, but we feel that passion for you—and we need to believe that you feel the same way about us.

9. We think and feel deeply.

It's generally accepted that men don't have feelings. That's what we might call an "urban legend." Men know what they think and feel, but they might be slower than women to express it. It's in there, though, and it's real. Women need to recognize it and handle it carefully. Those emotions are fragile because of past experiences.

Growing up, boys are told (sometimes by parents, always by peers) that they're not supposed to cry. They don't get a lot of unconditional acceptance for their feelings as they mature, so they've trained themselves to not show emotion.

In a safe relationship with a woman, they'll probably let their guard down. In a sense, they're sticking their toes in the ocean to see how cold it is. If a man tells a woman he's afraid, he's watching and waiting to see how she responds. If it's safe, he'll feel ok with being vulnerable in the future with her. If it's not safe, he'll keep turning inward.

We have real fears. Don't try to talk us out of them. Just listen to us—not to agree with us or fix us, but to understand us and stand by us. Reassure us that you're walking through the fear with us so we're not facing it alone. When a man gets understanding from a woman, it's a rare gift.

10. We need your respect and admiration.

Respect is one of a man's greatest needs. When a woman shows a man that she believes in him and his ideas, it makes him feel important. Sure, we come up with some crazy ideas. But instead of focusing on why the ideas won't work, explore them with us. Encourage the way we think and our energy around doing something big, even if you're concerned about what's involved.

If you respect us for the way we think, we'll feel your support. If we feel supported, we'll feel secure enough to give up the crazy ideas over time. We just need to know that you're on our side.

Notice when we're doing things well and tell us. We need "unconditional like," knowing that you respect us just for who we are. When you point those things out, it reinforces that feeling of respect.

11. We need your companionship.

We like you. If we're in a relationship with you, we want to be with you. Sometimes it means we want to have conversations, but it also means just being together watching a hockey game on television. Yes, we need independence, and we want time to hang out with the guys. But we also need time to just be with you. Sitting quietly together without talking recharges us, and we need it as much as conversation.

We didn't get into a relationship with you so we could be by ourselves. We want to know who you are in a simple, safe environment.

12. We need encouragement.

We can get "down" sometimes, but we don't always say anything about it. You can tell, though, because you're perceptive enough to notice that we're quieter than usual—we're not responding, we're not playing with the kids, or we don't want to go anywhere.

When you give us encouragement during those times, we feel like we can conquer any situation—and we'll do anything for you if you make that happen. When we get stuck in the weeds while we're trying to move forward, let us know you have our back. Your support makes it safer to try things, because you've given us a soft place to land if we mess up.

13. We need you to flirt with us.

We're suckers for flirting. When our confidence is low, playful flirting fills our emotional tank. A mischievous smile or a gentle, casual touch is the quickest way to bring that confidence back. It makes us feel alive, because you care enough to do it. Other women have a flirty style and approach, and it's attractive. But it's not nearly as attractive if we're already getting it from you.

14. We need appreciation.

We men play a lot of different roles, so it means a lot when you tell us we're doing a good job in those roles. We don't get a lot of recognition for what we do, which is why it means so much when we get it from you. When you notice that we've done something for you like clearing the table or filling your car with gas, just say thanks. Nobody likes to be taken for granted, and gratitude makes us want to do it again.

One of the most meaningful ways you can show appreciation is to do it behind our back. Brag on us to others when we're not around. It'll get back to us, and we'll experience the power of a secondhand compliment.

How to Speak Male (Part 1)

To connect effectively with your man, realize that he speaks a different language. If you speak to him the way you would talk to another woman, he might not be able to hear it. It's important to choose phrasing that makes sense to him.

If you want him to help, don't say, "I get so tired of cleaning up the kitchen." You're hoping he'll get the hint and help you out. He won't, because he thinks you're simply stating a fact. Ask directly. "Could you please help me by emptying the dishwasher tonight? I'd really appreciate it."

Share your emotions accurately instead of lacing them with sarcasm. Instead of saying, "You never listen to me. What's wrong with you?" try, "I really feel frustrated when I don't get a response from you when we're talking."

Instead of saying, "You're always out with your friends and leaving me home alone," try, "I'm glad you get a chance to hang out with your friends. I'll be going out with my friends tomorrow night. Why don't you have the guys over to watch the game together?"

He's used to hearing you say, "I love you." It's expected, and appreciated. Try saying, "You know, I really like you today." That's unexpected and catches his attention at a deeper level.

When you're busy and he knows it, take a break to just be with him. Say, "I have so much going on right now that I'm feeling overwhelmed. I just need a few minutes to be with my best friend, ok?" That's hard to resist.

How to Speak Male (Part 2)

"The definition of insanity," the adage goes, "is to keep doing the same thing over and over and expect different results."

If your current way of communicating isn't working with your man, it's probably time to evaluate how you're doing it. If you have an accurate idea of what's going on in his head, you can take some different approaches to connecting.

Let's give him the benefit of the doubt and say that he really cares about you and wants to please you. He doesn't know how to do that because he's tried and gotten a negative response. He feels like a failure and chooses inappropriate backup behaviors to protect himself.

Here are some communication strategies that will make it safe for him to respond differently.

Focus on solutions. If you focus on the way you're communicating, a man often feels threatened. Your brain puts things together faster than his, and he's going to withdraw. Instead, turn your attention to solving the problem together.

   After you've agreed on exactly what the problem is, say, "So I'd be interested to hear your take on this. What would you do?" When he tells you, don't react. Just listen and say, "Interesting. I hadn't looked at it that way. Let me think about that for a couple of minutes." That gives you time to consider his thoughts and choose the best way to respond next.

   If you disagree, don't tell him he's wrong. Just say, "You know, I've got another idea to add. Let's see if we can pull our ideas together to come up with something that will work." That lets you converse in a way that allows him to be a winner.

Don't bring up situations from the past. One of the biggest complaints I hear from men is how good a woman's memory is, and how she brings up things from the past to reinforce her position about the present. It's usually true, because a woman's greater production of dopamine increases her language and memory skills. Keep the present issue in the present and keep the past in the past. If the past needs to be addressed, that can happen later—not during the present conflict.

Keep it short. Men don't have as much stamina for a long, involved conversation. Even if the conversation is healthy, men tend to have a limit to how long they can stay engaged. If you see him start to talk less, glaze over, or lose interest, wrap it up and agree on when you can talk again. It's better for a man to have several short conversations than a single one that seems eternal.

Summarize. Your mind is probably looking at a situation from a number of different angles, and it makes sense to you how those different ideas all come together. A man tends to see one thing at a time and can get confused or overwhelmed when a conversation goes in too many directions. When you've been talking about your perspective for a while, see if you can summarize what you're thinking in a single sentence. Ask him if it makes sense. Then ask him to do the same: "So, what do you see as the bottom line?"

Remember who you're talking to. He's not the enemy. He's your best friend. It's a relationship that's worth keeping in perspective.

Let him know what you need. Men can't read minds, so it's important to let him know exactly what you need in a situation. If you just want him to be a sounding board, give him a time frame and let him know you don't need a solution. "Could you give me ten minutes to bounce around some stuff going on in my head? I don't need you to fix it, but it will help me feel supported if I know you hear me."

If you need him to look you in the eye about something you're feeling, tell him, "I've got something important I need your thoughts about. For this one, could you give me some eye contact, and then you can go back to the paper in about ten minutes?" If you want a solution, say, "I need some advice. Let me give you the options I'm thinking of, and then you can give me some direction."

Don't let him bring you down. If he's in a reactive or grumpy mood, don't go there with him. He might want you to wallow with him, but you'll both recover more easily if you stay in charge of your own moods.

Fitting the Situation

These are the things that break the stereotypes. They're the things that men overwhelmingly say are true, and they really want their women to know the truth. It isn't a rigid set of rules to follow; it's just a view into the hidden recesses of how a man thinks.

These will apply differently in different situations, but they will still apply. A dating relationship has different dynamics than a marriage. In dating, it helps a woman know how a man thinks as she's exploring the potential of a relationship. In marriage, it explains actions that show up over time that she might not have seen at the beginning. For a mom of a teenage son, it helps her to understand what he's thinking when he's going through the silent years.

Men appreciate when women look beyond the stereotypes. It means they're being treated like a real, whole person instead of a caricature.

PART 4

How He Communicates

I heard a woman say once that "male communication" was an oxymoron. If he's male, he can't communicate. If he communicates, he must not be male.

That's an unfair stereotype that can keep real communication from happening. Men usually have the capacity for amazing communication skills, but they look totally different from a woman's. Men have deep feelings but express them differently. They tend to go silent, but that doesn't mean they're disengaged.

It's tough for men because they know they've been stereotyped in the media as unfeeling, uncaring, and uncommunicative. They know it's not true, but they're not sure what to do about it.

In this section, we'll give those men a voice. Let's explore their motives and perspectives to find out how they really communicate.

It's a chance to become bilingual—to learn how to speak "male."

9

Do Guys Even *Have* Feelings?

Archie Bunker, the fictional husband and father from the seventies television show *All in the Family*, was the poster boy for negative stereotypes about men. Played by Carroll O'Connor, he was the gruff, bigoted stereotypical male who exemplified everything negative about men. The show was wildly popular, in part because so many women resonated with the stereotype.[1]

If it weren't for these perceptions, it would be a lot harder to come up with material for television comedies or movie story lines. No one questions if they're true or not. We just assume that they're accurate and the plot builds from there. We think, *Yeah, he's a typical guy.*

Of course, every guy is different. Some guys will be more like these stereotypes and some will be less. By exploring these perceptions, we'll find some principles we can apply to the vast majority of men, and good reasons behind those principles.

Before we determine if they're true or not, it will be helpful to revisit the male brain to see how it influences a man's emotions and actions.

What's Going On in His Head?

Earlier, we talked about the structural differences between a man's brain and a woman's brain. Women have more "white matter," the connective tissue that links the two hemispheres of the brain. Men have more "gray matter," which means they generally use a single section of their brain at a time. Women connect everything to everything, while men don't make those same connections.

In other words, we all have the same way of taking information in (through the senses), but we process it very differently. Advances in brain imaging have allowed researchers to study those differences and see exactly what takes place. Here are some of the recent discoveries that apply to a man and his emotions:

The left side of the brain contains our ability to process language. Men have fewer brain cells there, and the number of brain cells predicts performance. More brain cells means better performance. So if women have more cells there, it follows that they tend to be better at language and communication. The more they use those skills, the better they get—and that section of the brain actually grows.

Because of the larger amount of white matter in a woman's brain, she processes incoming information differently than a man. Single words are processed in the same way by both men and women, but sentences are processed differently. Men process information in a single, specific area on one side of the brain, while women utilize the same area on both sides of the brain. It also means that women can think and feel at the same time, while men tend to do so separately.

Women tend to use more of their brain to listen and speak. It doesn't mean they're better communicators; it just means communication tends to come easier for them.

Women have a greater supply of estrogen than men, which impacts the number of neurons used when they're upset. That's why women tend to experience stress more intensely than men. Estrogen also impacts learning and memory, so they hang on to information longer and better than men.

Women release the hormone oxytocin when they're under stress, which helps them bond with other people. Men release oxytocin too—but more often during hugs and sexual encounters. Women talk with others about their problems and feel better when they discuss solutions, gain empathy from others, and get input about their thoughts. Men don't typically have that chemical release, so they're not drawn to bringing others into their circle when they feel that pressure.

Men can identify more obvious emotions like anger and aggression in the facial expressions and body language of others but have trouble distinguishing more subtle cues such as worry and fear. Women usually pick up those signals more easily when they occur.[2]

The problem for communication comes when a woman processes things in a certain way because of her brain chemistry and assumes that her man should be doing the same thing. After all, the situation is the same—so why should he see it any differently? With that perspective, the logical conclusion is that the man is just being stubborn or lazy or unresponsive. He needs to work on his relational skills and just get better, right?

Wrong. It's not a behavior or character issue. It's a brain issue. As long as a woman feels the need to change the way a man operates, she's setting herself up for failure and frustration. Those differences are real, so she needs to find ways to capitalize on them.

If she doesn't, it's like moving into an apartment complex after owning a home. The apartment comes with a set of rules that seem to restrict one's freedom because homeowners can do whatever they want on their property. But an apartment has noisy neighbors, shared space, and regulations to make sure everyone gets along. That's the downside, and it's real. The upside is that when the toilet breaks or the stove doesn't work, somebody else takes care of it.

Relating to a man has a set of "rules" and might feel restrictive. Now it's two people to consider instead of just one, and there needs to be some change if these two are going to learn to partner together. The upside is that when problems arise, you don't have to face them alone.

It's not a matter of which one is better; it's about weighing the differences and adjusting to them. That's why a relationship between a man and a woman isn't about who's right and who's wrong; it's about valuing the differences and finding ways to work as a team, joining two perspectives into one.

Don't Believe the Media

Watch any sitcom or most talk shows, and you'll see a stereotype of men perpetuated as though it's "common knowledge." Men are assumed to be bumbling disasters in relationships. Women love them but have to control them to get anything done. Men are nice to have around and they have their strong moments, but they have to be coerced or manipulated into accomplishing anything. They're seen as emotionally clueless and don't know how to meet a woman's needs (or even desire to).

The other swing the media takes is portraying men as superheroes or ruggedly handsome leading men who take great risks to save the day and be the hero.

From the men I've talked to, neither one could be further from the truth.

A man does want to be a hero and save the day—but primarily for the most important woman in his life. He knows he won't be rescuing a galaxy from destruction but fantasizes about doing it at home. At the same time, he sees the sitcom caricatures of men and doesn't know what to say to counter it. "That's not me," he might say. "But how do I convince a woman that I'm different?"

Those caricatures of men turn into urban myths—things that are commonly believed but not accurate. Let's explore those myths to see what's under the surface.

Myths about Men

Let's revisit some stereotypes about men. They're common beliefs about men held by women (and even men) and can damage relationships if they're held on to for any length of time. That's why it's important to find out what's true in each case, so we can have an accurate perspective to work from.

Myth #1—Men don't have feelings.

This is the biggest myth of all, and the one that bothers men the most.[3] Men absolutely have feelings, and those feelings can be intense. Watch a baseball team win the World Series or a football team win the Super Bowl, and you'll see a display of emotion that's totally uninhibited. The team rushes together, hugs each other roughly, jumps up and down as a group, slaps each other on the back, and runs around the field in celebration. During the game itself, they can be fueled by emotion that drives their performance.

At the same time, men deeply feel the "softer" emotions like sadness, fear, worry, and sensitivity. In fact, most men have a large chunk of insecurity that's just below the surface and impacts the way they handle life.

Men have usually been brought up in a culture that tells them it's not masculine to show those softer emotions but it's ok to show the harder ones. Just because these feelings aren't obvious doesn't mean they don't exist. In fact, it's even tougher, because these men don't have the tools to express those emotions—so those emotions often get stuck inside. Sometimes men convert feelings like sadness into something more acceptable, like anger.

Men feel emotions deeply. They just don't always know what to do with them.

Myth #2—If men do have feelings, they don't want to talk about them.

Many men didn't grow up with a dad who was good at showing emotions, so they didn't have a model to learn from. They weren't raised to show vulnerability. They were taught to be strong, not needy.

Most men won't ask for directions. It's an extension of that desire to appear in control. They also don't want to admit that something hurt their feelings, because it makes them feel weak. A man will fight another man instead of telling him that he was hurt by his words.

Women tend to express their emotions verbally, while men tend to express their emotions physically. When they feel strong emotions, they often find physical outlets to express them such as lifting weights or playing violent video games. That's not necessarily why they engage in physical activity, but releasing the emotion becomes a fringe benefit.

Men will talk to other men about what they're feeling, but they keep it short and simple.[4]

"Man, I'm really bummed about what's happening with my in-laws," he'll say.

"Yeah," comes the response, "I hear you. Those relationships can be tough sometimes."

"Yep. I'm not sure what to do. Have you had trouble with your in-laws?"

"Oh, yeah. But we worked it out over time. It's tough to know what to do."

"I guess. Hey, did you watch the game last night?"

For a guy, that's all he needs or wants. But when he talks to a woman about what he's feeling, it's different. She wants to know the details of what he's feeling, but he doesn't even know them himself. If she presses to find out, he either withdraws and clams up or gets upset.

When a woman says she wants him to share his feelings, he's found it to be a selective request. She wants the soft emotions but not necessarily the hard ones. He doesn't have much experience with sharing those softer emotions, so he feels like she's forcing him to fly an airplane when he's only driven a car.

There's a concept we talked about earlier that's worth repeating: it's risky for a man to share his emotions with a woman, but he'll try if he trusts her. If she brushes him off, makes light of what he's feeling, or tries to force him when he's not ready, he won't try again. If she responds with safety, patience, and care for his emotions, he'll be more inclined to share more in the future.

Myth #3—Men don't understand women and don't want to try.

In 1995, Dr. Alan Francis published a 120-page book called *Everything Men Know about Women.*[5] It immediately became a bestseller and still sells well two decades later. Why did it become so popular?

The pages were all blank.

Men really do want to know what women think. But the process breaks down when a woman isn't clear about what she means and he can't figure it out. When she tells him directly, he understands. His nonconnective brain has trouble finding the hidden meaning behind her words.

He understands clearly what she's feeling when she says, "I'm feeling upset because we agreed not to spend anything until payday, because we had those extra expenses for car repairs. So when you bought that new video game, it was frustrating." But he can't make the connection if she says, "You're always spending money when we don't have it!" because he doesn't have all the information.

It's not that he doesn't want to understand. His brain just isn't wired to assign meaning when it's not direct. It's even harder when multiple issues are presented at the same time.

Myth #4—Men are more interested in their work than in their woman.

A woman says, "Why is your job so important to you?" To a man, she's hinting that it should be less important. He thinks, *Why wouldn't it be important?*[6]

A man finds a sense of validation and value in his work. The drive to succeed, conquer, provide, and "win" are wired into his brain, and he's spent a lifetime trying to become successful at his work. With that much effort, he's looking for a strong return on his investment. When a man isn't able to work, his self-esteem is at risk. He wants to make a contribution that matters. He wants to make a difference.

Comparing the importance of his relationship with his woman and his job doesn't make sense to a man. He sees them in two totally different categories. To him, it would be like asking a child, "Did you walk to school, or did you carry your lunch?" The question is nonsensical.

If a man is unsuccessful in either category, it impacts his performance in the other. A man's work takes a lot of time and energy, but it doesn't mean he's more interested in it than in his woman. It will take constant attention to find the balance between those two commitments. That's what takes the most energy—loving both, and trying to give each the attention they deserve.

Myth #5—Men are afraid of commitment.

Single women often feel like men have a fear of commitment. To a man, that implies he doesn't take his relationship seriously, desiring all the fun but none of the responsibility. It usually bothers a man to be seen as that frivolous because he knows the opposite is usually true. Several studies have shown that men are more likely than women to prefer marriage over being single for life, and are equally desirous of a strong family connection.[7]

The issue isn't fear of commitment; it's more about timing. They're not in a rush to make a lifelong commitment because they want to be sure they're making the right choice. Once they find the right woman and make that decision, they tend to be in it for the duration. It's that long-term focus that makes them cautious of pulling the trigger.

Men take longer to study a potential relationship before committing to it because they want to see what the relationship will be like over time. They innately understand the "honeymoon stage" of any relationship, and want to move past that to see how she will handle real-life issues with him.

In other words, most men want commitment, and they want it long-term. So they take their time to get it right.

Myth #6—Men don't listen.

A man's brain processes information differently than a woman's brain.[8] Most men want to know what their woman thinks about things. Men tend to be succinct, while women tend to provide details.

When men hear intricate details of a woman's conversation with her friend, they try to organize it into bullet points in their minds. If there are too many details to sort, their mind tends to freeze up and they can't take in more information. It's like a computer that locks up and has to be restarted before it can continue processing.

Women *need* to share the details. Men don't always understand that, so they tune out when they can't process all those details. To a woman, that comes across as not listening or caring.

My wife will have lunch with a friend whom she hasn't seen for a while. That evening I'll ask her, "So, how did it go at lunch today?" Typically, she'll start at the beginning and tell me everything they talked about, how each of them responded, and what she felt about each part of the conversation. It might take ten minutes or more to describe that lunch meeting.

I go to lunch with a friend I haven't seen for a while, and Diane says, "Tell me about your lunch today." I usually say, "It was good. He's doing good." She says, "Well, what did you talk about?" I search my brain for clues, but it's blank. I spent an hour with my friend and don't know what we talked about—at least not in detail. Since the conversation is done, I've filed those details away in my mental archives. The conversation is over and we're done talking, so I don't keep the details in current memory.

Over the years, Diane and I have learned what each other needs in conversation. When she goes into great detail about a conversation, I've learned to listen and let her talk. I don't do it because the details are important to me. I do it because *she's* important to me. When I listen, it draws us together.

At the same time, she's learned not to feel hurt because I'm not sharing details about my lunch conversations. She knows that I'm not going to have much to contribute. Her brain makes all the connections of everything that happened. My brain focuses on the other person during lunch, and then it moves on to something else.

I'm not the norm in regard to listening to her details. It's been a long, slow learning curve for me, and I realize that most men aren't there yet. I still get impatient sometimes because I'm looking for bullet points. But I also know that Diane and I get stronger, together, when we allow each other to be who we are. It became easier for me to listen once I realized how important it was to her.

When a man is listening in silence, it doesn't mean he's bored. It probably means he's listening more deeply, because the energy it takes for a man to listen makes it hard for him to respond at the same time. If he doesn't answer right away, it's because he needs time to think before responding.

A woman can bring that up during a comfortable conversation as something to explore together. "Can you help me think through something? When I'm telling you something I'm thinking about, you don't say much back. I used to think it's because you weren't listening. But I'm wondering if it means you're actually listening more but processing it inside your head. I'd love to hear your perspective."

Myth #7—Men never tell a woman they care about her.

Men use actions more than words to express their feelings.[9] They want to be romantic, but don't always find it natural to use words to do it. They feel inadequate and embarrassed at saying romantic things (especially when they compare them-selves with leading men on television), and they're afraid of doing it wrong. So they use actions instead.

If a man sends flowers, it's his way of expressing his feel-ings. Men don't usually send flowers out of guilt (though it happens). It's their way of saying "I love you" or "I'm sorry" or "I was thinking about you" without having to say the words. When he plans a trip with you, it's because he wants to be with you. When he gets your car fixed, it's because he wants to do something to make your life easier and take care of you.

Don't overlook these actions, assuming that they're not as valid as a verbal expression. Savor the words when they come, but recognize the reality of his actions as an expres-sion of his heart.

Myth #8—When a woman is upset, men are worthless.

Some man said, "Women don't want you to put out the fire; they just want you to stand with them in the fire while they burn." Men want to put out the fire. Women don't want to face the fire alone. A healthy relationship draws from both perspectives to build a lasting connection.

Men care when a woman is upset, but they usually have no idea what to do. They want to fix things but they don't have the right tools to fix emotions.

When a woman is upset, it adds stress to the relationship if she assumes that her man doesn't care because he's not meeting her needs at the moment. A better option is to give him tools. She can tell him what she needs and ask for it in a way he can understand.

When he sees you crying and doesn't know how to respond, give him a suggestion. "I'm crying because (describe in one sentence what happened). I don't need you to fix it. But I need you to come and hold me for a few minutes—then we'll go out to lunch."

You'll get what you need, and you'll give him a way to help you solve the problem. It's a synergistic way to work as a team.

It's a perfect example of a win-win solution.

10

The Silent Partner

My son, Tim, speaks fluent Spanish. He's been involved in restaurant management since graduating from college, and his first exposure to the language was while working in a restaurant kitchen. When he started managing a restaurant in San Diego, all of his workers were Hispanic. He learned the conversational basics because he needed to communicate with them.

He cared about them and wanted to understand their culture as well as their language. So he left that job and moved to Mexico for about six months to take intensive language immersion classes. There he learned proper structure and usage so he would have a solid foundation to build on.

After the classes ended, he stayed for a few more months and did volunteer maintenance work at a Christian conference center. That gave him a chance to live among the people and speak their language every day. That experience enabled him to become fluent.

We decided to start learning Spanish when Tim fell in love with Lucy, a girl he met at that conference center and married five years later. The wedding was in Guadalajara, so we wanted to be able to communicate with her family and friends when we went. We bought Spanish language CDs and began to listen.

We learned a few words and phrases, and it gave us the chance to connect with our new family members. It was a great start and enabled us to communicate at the most basic level. It probably gave them a few chuckles as well. But we're definitely not fluent.

Tim is fluent in Spanish because he lived among people who spoke it and now he speaks with his restaurant staff every day. We've only listened to CDs, so it hasn't become part of us. I asked a bilingual friend once, "How do you know that you're fluent in another language?" He said, "When you dream in that language."

Communicating with the Deaf

When it comes to communicating with men, it often feels like you're speaking a foreign language. You say one thing and they hear something else. You try to connect with each other, but "connect" turns into "disconnect."

Men and women care about each other, so they want to find a solution to a problem that has come up. Because of the way their brains work, they choose different paths to find it. Women tend to *talk* toward a solution, using words to figure out what's happening. Men tend to *think* toward a solution, often going silent because they don't know what to say. They don't know how to respond to their woman's questions, so they just stop talking.

Both people want a solution but approach it in different ways. If they don't understand those differences, they both end up frustrated.

We've heard of the man who is the "strong, silent type." Old Western movie stars like John Wayne and Clint Eastwood fit that stereotype. They didn't say much but their strong presence and actions provided a mystique that sent women swooning in theaters.

While a woman may be attracted by that quiet strength, she's often disappointed as the relationship progresses. "He never talks to me," she says. "He won't let me in."

Silence becomes a default language for many men. For some, it's occasional. For others, it has become a pattern. For everyone, silence stops communication in its tracks. When we don't know what the other person is thinking, we tend to fill in the blanks from our own perspective. We assume they're thinking the same thing we're thinking.

They're not thinking the same thing.

If a woman is going to communicate effectively with a man, she needs to become bilingual. She needs to learn the language of silence, and how to connect with her man when he uses it.

Why Men Stop Talking

There are reasons why men tend to go silent. Some of those reasons are intentional, while others happen without him realizing it. Not all of them are rational, but they're real.

He doesn't know how to respond. When a woman asks a
man what he's thinking about a situation, he might
not have thought through it yet. If it happened earlier, his mind has probably moved on to something
else—so it's off his radar. He feels the pressure to
come up with a response but doesn't know what
to say.

Since his brain focuses on fewer things at a
time, he has trouble keeping up. He doesn't want
to appear incompetent, so he just stops talking.
Over time it becomes his coping strategy and turns
into his default setting. It means he's run out of
options.

He feels attacked. When a man feels pressured to say
something but doesn't know what to say, he feels
like he's the prey in a big game hunt. He feels
like the woman has the weapons and he's naked
and defenseless. That's the opposite of how his
mind works, since he's wired for winning and
success. In this case, silence becomes a mask for
his fear.

He's an introvert. We'll talk about this more in the next
chapter. While introverts tend to think deeply, they
can't do it out loud. They take in information and
then need time to think about it alone. Once they've
processed, they can share their thoughts. Trying to
rush their thinking is as futile as expecting a car to
run without gas.

He doesn't connect information quickly. Because of the
combination of connective brain tissue and higher

estrogen levels, women can "build a case" more quickly around any issue. They have access to their memory in a way that allows them to combine experiences to make their point. Men sometimes feel intimidated or helpless because they can't come up with responses that are as sophisticated or as quick. So they simply shut down as a defense.

He's been taught that "silent" means "masculine." Men have been conditioned by the media that showing feelings and talking about them isn't masculine. It also comes from peers growing up, where friends made fun of him if he shared too much. So when he gets into a relationship with a woman, he's afraid the woman won't like him if he isn't masculine. He shuts up to keep that from happening.

He needs to win, and silence helps. If a man feels like he's not going to be successful in a conversation with a woman, he'll go quiet to avoid defeat. It seems irrational because the woman might not even know they're in a battle. He doesn't either, and he's not trying to "beat" you in the discussion. He needs to feel that the outcome of the dialogue is a win-win situation where he feels successful at the end.

He wants to respect you. In a relationship, most men want to show respect to a woman. If they were taught that growing up, it's the filter they work from (though some men were brought up with a different filter). Even if there's anger in a conversation, they still want to treat a woman with respect. That's

tough if he feels pressure to explain his position before he has thought it through, because he doesn't
want to say something impulsive he'll later regret.
So he goes quiet as a way of protecting the relationship.

He wants you to be happy. Everyone has heard the
old line, "If Mama ain't happy, ain't nobody
happy." It's an unfortunate stereotype that pic-
tures an angry woman taking out her emotions on
everyone around her while her man remains quiet.
Men genuinely want to give their best for their
woman.

He *does* want to make you happy—not out of
fear of your response when you're upset but because
he genuinely cares about you. He wants his woman
to know how deeply he's affected by her moods. If
she's not happy, he's not happy. Silence becomes an
unknowing strategy to avoid pain. If he doesn't talk,
he won't risk upsetting her. It's often inappropriate,
but common.

Being silent has become a habit. When he doesn't have
other resources, a man scrambles to find whatever
solution works. If silence is the solution that works
on a regular basis, he doesn't just choose it anymore
. . . it has become a habit.

Learning to Speak Male

If you speak to me in English but I only speak Spanish, I
won't understand what you're trying to communicate. Even

if I want to, I can't—because I don't have a clue what you're talking about. I can't tell if you're giving me information, asking questions, or seeking input. I'm confused. So, what do I do? I remain silent.

My silence doesn't mean I'm being obstinate or irrational or stubborn or that I'm "just being a man." I simply don't understand what you're saying. If you try to read into my motives, you're making assumptions about my silence—and those assumptions are probably wrong.

If we want to connect, there are only two options:

1. I can learn English.
2. You can learn Spanish.

Sure, it would be nice if I would learn English, and it would be easier to converse with you. But as a male, I think it sounds like a lot of work. I'd have to be convinced that the payoff would be worth the effort.

This sounds unfair, because my relationship with you should be enough motivation, right? Why should you have to be the one who becomes bilingual?

But if you learn even a few phrases in Spanish, we can begin to connect. I'll enjoy that connection and recognize its value. As a result, I'll be much more inclined to pick up my English CDs and begin the process myself. In other words, I'll get motivated if you take the first step.

It's a guy thing.

Besides taking that initiative, there are other things that can make bilingual communication easier. For example, it's important to know that men aren't wired to remember details about a conversation they've had. Women get together for an hour and know each other's tastes in decorating, background, child-rearing philosophies, and hobbies. Men spend four hours together driving to the river and back, and spend two nights in the same tent, and can't remember anything they talked about.

Men share experiences, not words. That's their language. That means that it's more natural to express their love and care for their woman by doing things for her rather than telling her. He might express his feelings for her, but not as often as she might like.

We talked about this in an earlier chapter, but it's worth repeating. Knowing that men express their care in actions more than words, a woman needs to be a keen observer of the things he does for her. If he brings her tea in bed or washes her car on a Saturday morning to surprise her, she needs to recognize that it's his way of saying, "I love you." An appropriate response (that makes him want to repeat that action in the future) is to respond in the same appreciative way she would if he had formed the actual words.

Talking Tips

Cross-cultural communication involves being intentional in conversation. If you want to connect with your man in a language he can understand, here are a few "grammar" tips.

Slow down.

Men usually take more time to process information than women, since women's brains are wired to make multiple connections quickly. Men tend to have more of a single-focus approach, and you'll lose him quickly if you go too fast.

Remember that when a man doesn't respond right away, it doesn't mean he's disengaged. In fact, it might even mean that he's *more* engaged and is taking the time to listen carefully and process before responding. Give him the freedom to take more time to put his thoughts into words than it would take you to do the same.

If you find yourself feeling impatient because of his slow response time, pause and give him space. Don't fill the silence; just wait for him to speak. That silence can feel like a vacuum, so you need to resist the pressure to fill the void too quickly.

You might think, *Yes, but that takes a lot more time.* That's true. One of the biggest relationship killers is when people try to rush their conversations. Being efficient with people almost always slows down the process of connection. Real trust is built in real relationships, and real relationships take time to grow. Deep, meaningful relationships develop in a crockpot, not a microwave.

Rushing a relationship is like expecting a toddler to do calculus. It's not that he's incapable; there's a learning curve, so it will just take him a while to get there.

Don't try to fix his silence issues when emotions are high.

Logic and emotion go together like oil and water. When you're in a discussion where emotions are high, it's the wrong time to try to address the deeper issues in a relationship. Those strong feelings rob us of our ability to be objective, and we end up saying things we regret or making accusations that break down real communication. It's not just a "guy thing" or a "woman thing." It's a relationship thing.

If your house is on fire, it's the wrong time to argue about who left the stove on. You might win the argument, but you'll lose the house. Deal with the crisis at hand and talk about its causes later.

If your man is frustrating you with his silence, forcing him to respond will usually just escalate the problem. A more effective approach would be to acknowledge how his silence is impacting you and suggest a neutral time to explore his reasons for it.

You could say, "You know, I'm really frustrated right now because we're trying to work through this issue and I feel like you're not participating. It's important to me, and I want to know what you're thinking." That approach is honest, and you're demonstrating the respect he needs. You're not accusing him; you're just telling him what you're feeling and letting him know you value his thoughts.

If you want to explore his thinking, do so in a way that works for him instead of just for you. Don't say, "Can we sit down and talk about this sometime?" To him, that feels like he's being called into the principal's office. Instead, say, "Can we go to Starbucks (or someplace else he really likes to go) and talk about this sometime?" That keeps the conversation on a more casual plane and feels a lot less threatening. You're going somewhere that he enjoys, which makes him feel "liked" and respected. In that setting, there's a much better chance he'll open up about why he goes silent during your conversations.

When he tells you what he's thinking, just listen. Don't become defensive or probe beyond where he takes it. Let him talk. If he doesn't feel pressured, he'll give you some valuable information. Don't try to get everything at once. Let him share a little, then go back to Starbucks a few weeks later for another round. You've just made it safe for him, which is exactly what he needs to share his thoughts.

Give him permission to postpone.

This is an extension of the previous suggestion. You won't make much progress by forcing him to respond immediately. During one of those neutral Starbucks conversations, let him know you recognize his need to process. Then decide on a way to let that happen that will work for both of you and will allow you to reconnect later.

One couple I know have agreed that when he doesn't know what to say, he simply says, "thirty minutes" or "one hour." She agrees to postpone the discussion for that time period, and he promises they will come back to it. It works for both of them because it meets both of their needs. They've also found that during this break, emotions dissipate and their discussion becomes more respectful.

Another version would be to postpone the discussion for a few days. You could say, "I know you need time to think, and it's really important to me that we don't let this slide. Can we revisit this in a couple of days after you've had a chance to think it through?" It still might not be comfortable for him, but you're approaching him in a way that respects him and his needs.

Ask for what you want.

Men are wired to find solutions to problems. If you're looking for a solution, ask him directly what he thinks you should do (he'll love that). If you're just bouncing around ideas and need to think through them aloud, tell him so. "I'd like your input on something," you could say. "I need to think through some options I have on this. Can you let me talk through them with you to help me sort out my thoughts? I'm not looking for a solution, but it would really help me if I could get your ideas."

That approach meets his drive to be needed and respected without jumping to a quick solution. Once you've talked, you might ask for his input about the best solution if it feels appropriate. You might actually want to hear it because he took time to listen instead of just "fix."

> **Don't ask him what he feels. Ask him what he thinks.**

He knows how to answer the second question, but not the first. You'll get the same information, but you've presented it in his language.

Learn to Listen to the Silence

One of the biggest frustrations women have is when their man won't talk. It's easy to feel like a man is being stubborn and uncommunicative and to begin to see him through that lens. That's why the stereotype has grown out of proportion.

The solution isn't to try to get men to talk more. It's to become a student of their language and communication styles, and capitalize on that uniqueness. If men are allowed to process information in a male way instead of feeling obligated to speak in a female way, they have the potential to be the best communicators ever.

They'll become the strong, silent type who knows how to connect to a woman's heart.

11

Conflict without Combat

The internet is filled with quotes about anger.

Telling an angry person to calm down is like trying to baptize a cat.

Never go to bed angry; stay up and plot your revenge.

You think I'm cute when I'm angry? Well, get ready—because I'm about to be gorgeous.

Anger is the feeling that makes your mouth work faster than your mind.

Most of these quotes are clever but don't provide much in the way of solutions—not that we expect them to. More surprising is the fact that there hasn't been a lot of research about handling conflict in relationships—at least not in comparison to all the other relationship topics.

That's unfortunate, because it's a universal issue. We've all experienced it in ourselves and others. When it happens in a relationship we deeply care about, we need some tools to sort it all out.

Hanging out with an angry person can be exhausting. There's a lot of energy around them, and it can be draining. If we're trying to engage in conversation with them, it wears us out. After a while we feel the need to step away from the emotion and "chill."

If it's a man who's angry, it can be even more challenging. Women are making all of these mental connections because of how their brains are wired, and they're trying to look at all the dynamics involved. Men use that single-focus aspect of their brain to see an irritating situation for what it is— irritating. They don't usually analyze what the offending person is doing or saying; they just get upset and assume the person needs to get their act together.

Someone offered this pithy summary of a man's typical response to anger: "I wouldn't have to manage my anger if people could learn to manage their stupidity." If someone upsets them, they simply assume the other person is the problem.

We all get angry. It's a human emotion, and we're all human. So when someone says, "Oh, don't get so angry," they're really saying, "Oh, stop being so human."

When anger happens in a relationship, it's usually the product of conflict. Two people have different opinions about something. If it's important enough, they try to work it out. But if both people think they're right, they don't want the other person's opinion. Instead, they feel obligated to convince the other person that they're wrong and need to change. The result? Somebody gets angry.

Conflict isn't a bad thing unless it pushes two people apart. When that happens, anger grows and barriers are built over time. But in its simplest form, conflict happens when two people grow together. If they're committed to the relationship, healthy conflict is a strategy for growth.

By that definition, a relationship without conflict is a stagnant relationship. Someone said that if two people agree on everything, one of them is unnecessary. It's not a matter of figuring out who's right and who's wrong. It's a process of drawing from those differences and looking for creative solutions that gain from the best of each person's perspective.

It's conflict without combat.

Different Approaches to Conflict

Darrel is fighting with his wife, Connie, over a bottle of salad dressing. She'd asked him if he needed anything at the store, and he'd said, "Ranch dressing." She brought home a bottle of "light" dressing instead of the "real" thing. She figured it would be the same but save calories.

"Are you crazy?" he yelled. "That's not ranch dressing. It tastes like chemicals. If I had wanted fake ranch dressing, I would have asked for fake ranch dressing." She was hurt because she was just trying to keep them healthy. He was upset because she didn't do what he expected.

First he was yelling. Then he went silent and disappeared to watch a game on TV. She tried to get him to talk about it, but he was too angry to respond. They had come to a communication impasse—over salad dressing.

She doesn't know what to do, so she calls her best friend, Linda, and discusses the situation. Linda listens and says, "Let me send Matt over to talk to him. They like to hang out— maybe he can get him to talk."

Matt tells Linda, "Are you crazy? Not a chance. That's their problem, not ours. Let it go."

It's a good example of what the research shows: men and women respond differently to conflict. Women use their connective brain tissue to come up with a number of strategies for resolving conflict. If they can't figure out how to get their man engaged in solving the issue, they'll go to friends for support and conversation. They're always thinking about how another person is feeling, so they feel driven to work it out as quickly as possible. When her man won't cooperate, she feels a sense of despair.

A man often feels powerless in a conflict with a woman, because he doesn't have as many "weapons" for the battle. She's making different connections to find solutions, and presents them one after the other. With his single focus, he doesn't have that many options and doesn't feel adequate to compete at her level. His brain is focused more on winning and status, so he defaults to strong emotion as his primary weapon.

While we've all experienced the different ways men and women handle conflict, there has never been any definitive proof that one way is better than another. They're just different. Avoiding conflict isn't the issue, because it's the foundation for growth in a relationship. When a couple can't talk about issues together, they both become more dissatisfied with their relationship.

The real issue is learning how to communicate during conflict in a way that attacks the issue instead of each other.

If two people can learn to work together toward that end, they have the potential to build communication skills that can handle the toughest situations.

No one ever looks good trying to make the other person look bad. Relationships are about working together, not pulling apart.

Finding a Model for Understanding Men during Conflict

"He's just being a guy. That's just the way they are."

It's a common way to stereotype men. That perspective assumes that:

1. All men share certain characteristics.
2. Those characteristics are negative.
3. Women just have to live with those negative characteristics, because men are stubborn and won't change.

It's true that it's tough for anyone to change. But lumping all men under the same umbrella robs women of the ability to find their man's uniqueness and build on it.

Over the years, researchers have developed different models to sort people out in an attempt to understand them better. These models use descriptions, colors, animals, and other examples to label these approaches. Most of them can be beneficial when applied in different situations.

As I researched this chapter, I tried to decide which model would provide the most value for women as they try to understand men. Though different ones were helpful, I didn't find any that worked well across the board. I decided a better approach was to look at two different models, which use simple observations about men that could help women the most during conflict.

One has to do with the way a man *responds*, while the other deals with his basic *temperament*. Mixing and matching these categories won't provide absolute answers, and they aren't designed to understand everything there is to know about men. They are specifically related to the different ways men handle conflict situations.

Two Different Responding Styles

First, let's look at how men respond. One consistent pattern I saw in the research was that most men tend to be driven by either anger or fear in the way they respond to different situations. Men who are driven by *anger* encounter a frustrating situation and their level of emotional energy begins to rise. They have a mindset that naturally moves them forward, toward those tough conversations. They don't back down, and their desire to conquer is stimulated. Emotional energy increases and provides the fuel for their thinking and responding.[1]

Men who are driven by *fear* when encountering the same situation also experience an increase in their level of emotional energy. But it's a different kind of energy, moving them away from the conflict. It puts them in a defensive mindset instead of an offensive mindset, and they worry about all the bad things that could result from this dialogue. It's pessimistic. They avoid conflict, so it's easier for them to back off because it's too uncomfortable. They focus on fear of the negative possibilities, and that focus turns inward.

Angry people move *forward* into conflict. Fearful people move *backward* away from conflict.

Two Different Temperament Styles

At the same time, there are two different temperament styles that apply: *introverts* and *extroverts.* I've written about these in previous books, because temperament style is such a simple way to understand someone's motivations for what they do.

"Introverted" isn't the same as "shy." I'm an introvert, but a noisy one. I talk for a living and am surrounded by people all day, every day. But when I'm around people, I'm using up energy. I enjoy being with them but find myself running out of steam the longer we're talking. At a certain point, I have to pull away by myself to recharge. Introverts gain energy when they're alone and exercise it when they're with people.

Extroverts can be either outgoing or quiet, but they recharge when they're with others. They gain energy by being with people and lose energy if they spend too much time alone. They process their ideas by talking about them aloud, while introverts process their ideas when they're alone. To state it simply, introverts think *before* speaking, and extroverts think *by* speaking.

Extroverts often have trouble understanding the reflective nature of an introvert, and think they would get along much better in relationships if they could just be "healed" of their quiet approach. Introverts don't just *prefer* to process alone; it's the only way they can do it.

Put an introvert and an extrovert together in a relationship, and it provides some challenging dynamics. Learning to respect and value the other person's temperament is one of the most important tasks for anyone who wants a successful relationship. For women, it's one of the quickest ways to understand and connect with a man on his own terms.

Four Categories

Combine the two response styles and the two temperaments, and we can design a four-box grid of broad categories:

1. Anger-driven extroverts
2. Fear-driven extroverts
3. Anger-driven introverts
4. Fear-driven introverts

It's almost impossible to put a man squarely in the middle of any one quadrant. This isn't a scientific model to compete with others that are already out there. It's just a simple tool to help guide our thinking as we determine a man's motives and how to deal with them.

1. Anger-driven extroverts

These men can come across as aggressive and assertive. A woman can feel attacked by this combination, because it's forceful and direct. This describes a man who moves toward the conflict, not backing down from his position. He's often not a good listener because he's spending so much time talking. It can be frustrating dealing with him because he seems more concerned about being right than being connected.

	ANGER	FEAR
EXTROVERT	ANGER-DRIVEN EXTROVERT	FEAR-DRIVEN EXTROVERT
INTROVERT	ANGER-DRIVEN INTROVERT	FEAR-DRIVEN INTROVERT

Extroverts think by talking. That doesn't mean he firmly believes what he's saying. He might, but it's more likely that he's experimenting with ideas aloud. It's important to avoid feeling intimidated by him, which is easier to do when you recognize what's really going on. You won't change that combination, but you can work with it by understanding him. Realize that what he's saying firmly right now might not be the bottom line of his final decision and could change tomorrow.

Since he's thinking aloud, engage with him and ask questions about what he's saying. Don't react strongly to his thinking because it's still in formation. Your questions of exploration will help him shape his thinking.

2. Fear-driven extroverts

These men can seem like they're saying, "The sky is falling!" because of their approach. They're rehearsing everything that could possibly go wrong and could easily spiral downward into negative patterns of thinking. It's easy for a woman to become a rescuer in this situation because she's worried about his downward-spiraling, irrational thoughts.

In this case, his thoughts are being formed as he speaks. They haven't been shaped over time. They're impulsive ideas or even dreams that are expressed the moment they form in his head, and he might state them as though he's committed to whatever he said. Be careful not to let him drag you down emotionally, and don't immediately use logic to counter his arguments when he's feeling that strong emotion. That type of approach focuses on issues instead of relationship and drives him to think of more reasons to justify his thinking.

Listen empathetically, and focus more on what he's feeling and expressing than on sorting out the validity of what he's saying. Skip the actual issues until a more neutral time, and just say, "It sounds like you're really feeling concerned about this whole thing . . . am I right?"

3. Anger-driven introverts

These men need space to think. They can feel deep emotion during a conflict but haven't figured out what to say yet. The primary emotion they display is often frustration, which is frequently expressed as an irritated silence. Their anger drives them to deal with the situation, but they're frustrated because their thoughts don't make sense to them yet. Their feelings are real, but they don't know how to put them into words while the conflict is taking place. If you try to talk them through those feelings or ideas too quickly, they can get even more frustrated.

Acknowledge the frustration without trying to push for a response. Let him know that you recognize how strongly he's feeling and give him space to think. "I can tell you're really frustrated," you could say, "and you really have some strong feelings about this. I'd love to know what you're thinking, but I'm guessing you probably need some time to process it all. Is that right?"

That approach makes him feel safe, both in what he's feeling and in not knowing what he's thinking. It gives him permission to process without pressure. When he's feeling that safety, it's fair to ask him to share after he's had time to process. "Can we talk some more about this tonight after you've had a chance to think through the whole thing? I really value your perspective, and it would mean a lot to deal with this together."

4. Fear-driven introverts

These men can be tough to deal with unless you know what's happening. He turns inward, so you don't have the visible signs to sort through. Since he doesn't like conflict, he tends to avoid it. He doesn't want to fight with you, and bringing up his feelings might risk conflict. So he figures he needs to deal with it alone instead of facing the issue together. Picture a turtle pulling his head back into his shell for protection.

Remember: he hasn't had time to process his thoughts. If you press for information before he's ready, he'll withdraw.

From your perspective, it might look like he's disengaging and doesn't care. That can be frustrating because you feel like nothing will happen without you forcing it to happen. There's no input coming from his side.

In reality, there's plenty of energy. It's just turned inward instead of outward. Your best approach is to recognize what's happening, then provide an environment that feels safe to him. He needs to feel that you're not trying to take control of his behavior but rather reassuring him of your respect and partnership. "I can tell this is important to you, and you probably need time to sort it out, right?" you could say. "I know that usually helps you clarify what you're thinking. Just remember, you don't have to fix this alone. We're a team. How about if we both take some time to think through the whole thing, then grill some steaks and go for a walk after dinner to compare notes?"

Strategies for Solid Connection

These aren't foolproof descriptions and techniques that will automatically resolve every conflict you have in your relationship with your man. They're designed to help you be intentional as you interact. Your heart enables you to be empathic, which is priceless. Your head enables you to lead with your man's language instead of your emotions during a conflict situation.

It's easy to be reactive when your man responds differently than you during conflict. But if you become a student of that man, conflict can become a trigger for you to respond to the reality of who he is. Learn his uniqueness and focus on working together on issues instead of on each other.

The key to communicating with a man during conflict? Be intentional about leading with your head, not your emotions. If you lead with your heart, you'll mess with his head. If you lead with your head, you'll speak to his heart.

Men are wired for winning, but it doesn't have to be at your expense. "Win-win" can be just as satisfying to them as "I win." Deep inside, men want to be there for you. He entered a relationship with you because he values you. He wants you to win, but not if it means that he loses. If you respect the drive he has to win, he'll join you in the journey.

Here are a few simple strategies that provide safety for a man during conflict:

Don't back him into a corner and force him to express what he's feeling. Give him space to process and he'll usually let you in.

Be concise when talking during conflict. If there are too many words, a man feels overwhelmed and can't focus. He feels like he's in a foxhole and there are shots being fired from every direction. If that happens, he won't let you in his foxhole.

Use "I" messages when you're sharing your thoughts rather than "you" messages. Saying, "You always clam up when we talk" makes a man feel attacked. "When our conversation stops I feel frustrated" is more accurate and keeps him off the defensive. Instead of saying, "You just don't get it, do you?" say, "I wish I could express this more clearly."

Be careful not to imply that he *is wrong.* Focus on *what* is wrong. He might be wrong, but will never admit it if he's accused.

Don't multitask during conflict. You can probably clean
the kitchen while you're working through a tough
issue with your man, but he'll feel like you're distracted. His simple wiring that focuses on one thing
at a time might mean that he needs your eye contact.
If you're not sure, ask him if it would be helpful if
you just sat and connected.

*At the same time, most men don't do well just sitting and
having a "serious" conversation.* It's safer if he's doing
something like walking with you or going out for
dessert. Sometimes he'll express his thoughts more
easily when you're walking together because it's
active—and he doesn't have to look you directly in
the eye. Taking a drive together often accomplishes
the same result.

Watch his eye contact. Extroverts tend to make good eye
contact when they're talking but poor eye contact
when they're listening (so it looks like they're not listening). Introverts are the opposite; they make great
eye contact when listening but tend to look everywhere else when they're talking.

*Don't start tough conversations with something critical,
like "You never listen and we need to talk about
it."* Instead, bring up an issue in a way that assumes you want to handle it as a team. "I'd like
your input on something," you could start.
"Could I tell you what I'm thinking, and get your
thoughts? If I can hear what you're thinking, I
think we can figure something out that will work
for both of us."

Conflict marks a new stage of growth. It's not something to be avoided; we just need to understand what's happening with each other and make it a safe environment for healthy dialogue.

Always go for mutual benefit. It might seem like he wants to win at all costs. If that's happening, it's because you're approaching conflict as individuals—trying to determine who is right and who is wrong. Decide which battles are worth fighting and which ones you can agree to disagree about. For the real ones, always look for solutions that will satisfy both of you.

When you learn the skill of having conflict without resorting to combat, you're building a foundation for the rest of your relationship.

PART 5

How He Grows

When I was a kid, I loved to color.

Mostly I had coloring books, but I also just loved making stuff up on plain paper. I had a round, red-and-white tin box with a tight-fitting lid where I kept my crayons. Most of them were stubs with the labels torn off because they had been used so often. The ones in the best shape were mostly black, brown, and white—the colors I didn't use very often.

It was fun, but I always felt a bit limited in my creativity. When you only have a few colors, you can't create with a lot of variety.

One Christmas, my parents bought me a huge box of crayons. It was a flip-top Crayola box with at least one hundred different crayons. They lined up in their box in four different layers, all standing side-by-side as if to say, "Pick me! Pick me!"

I thought I was in heaven. Suddenly, I saw potential. With that many colors, I felt like I had options I had never seen before. I could make a whole new kind of picture with my new variety of choices.

A man's unique characteristics are like crayons. So are a woman's. In a lot of relationships, a couple spends their time comparing crayons to see who has the best ones. They'll argue about their opinions, trying to decide which color is best.

When that happens, they both have a lot of crayons but they don't share. If they can learn how to share, they both get to use an unlimited number of colors. Working together, they have the potential to create masterpieces.

It's easy to assume that men don't grow much. He is the person he will always be. When he's left alone, there's some truth to that.

But when he's in a dynamic relationship with a woman he cares about, he can grow into a person no one could have predicted. This section details that growth and the unique circumstances that build the seedbed that makes it happen.

Mostly, it happens when a man is in a growing relationship with a woman. Her influence and partnership provide the potential for a masterpiece.

12

The Lone Ranger in Relationships

R eal men don't eat quiche."
   That slogan became popular in 1982 through a book by the same name.[1] A number of other phrases spun off over the months that followed.

"Real men don't cry."

"Real men don't call other men 'just to talk.'"

"Real men don't eat fish at a steakhouse."

"Real men don't let a woman barbecue."

"Real men don't dust anything."

"Real men don't knit."

It was a reaction to the expansion of what was called the "Women's Movement," as women began to search for equality with men in pay, opportunity, political clout, and social standing. Up to that time, men were traditionally seen as leaders and women were seen as followers. Now, there was a quest for fairness.

Most men had a lot of self-assurance around those traditional roles and didn't know how to respond to this new paradigm. It reminded them of having a "boys only" treehouse when they were kids—and now the girls wanted to come in and decorate. Men were afraid of where that might lead. If women wanted to become more like men, men might be expected to become more like women.

This was outside their realm of thinking, and they weren't sure how to respond. With their simple, single-focus brains, they didn't know how to counter this new perspective without sounding like jerks. So they did the only thing they knew how to do: they came up with clever phrases to repeat (such as the ones above), challenging other men not to give up their masculinity.

Suddenly, men felt threatened. They loved their women but they also loved their role of protector and provider. They sensed that there was something right about not treating women like second-class citizens, but they felt pressure from society and the media to become less of a man in order to make that happen.

Instead of women rising to match the social level of men, equality seemed to mean that men had to come down and meet them halfway. To a man, it felt like women wanted to become more like men, and men were supposed to become more like women.

Nobody said that made sense, but that's how men saw it. It felt like relational socialism, where wealthy people had to share their wealth with poor people so everyone was equal.

As mentioned in chapter 1, the real problem was the terminology. "Equality" is different from "equal," and the terms were getting mixed up. "Equal" is when two things are exactly alike. In general, most things about men and women *are* alike. Our bodies all have skeletons, circulatory systems, hearts, and brains. But there are obvious differences in our reproductive systems. There are also general differences in our brains—how they're designed, how they work, and the hormonal differences that take place.

We're revisiting those differences because they're the starting point for understanding men. In this chapter, we'll talk about the reasons a man's relationships look so different from a woman's relationships. They impact all of his relationships—with himself, with other men, and with his woman.

The Sticking Points

Men aren't anti-female. They just have trouble understanding how females think, and don't know what to do with that. Most men haven't taken a course called "Women 101." They've spent their life having their most real conversations with other guys. (Ok, maybe with their mom too.)

Relating and communicating with a woman doesn't come naturally to him. It comes through trial and error (mostly error). Here's where it grows into a problem:

- He's wired to look and feel competent, so he won't ask for help (like not asking for driving directions).
- He won't ask women for help in understanding them because it would come across as not being competent. So he pretends he understands and wonders why it doesn't work out.

- He won't ask men for help in understanding women because he doesn't want to look incompetent in front of them, either. Since other men also don't understand women, they just talk about how hard it is to understand them.

Your man is stuck. He doesn't understand women and can't ask anyone. So he ends up trying to figure them out by himself.

It's not just women. Guys don't spend a lot of time trying to figure other men out, either. They enjoy hanging out together, but it's so they can do stuff without a lot of expectations. Their relationships are simple, and they don't explore each other's feelings deeply. They'll watch sports together or talk about work. As long as it's comfortable, they're ok. If it gets tense and they feel like the other person has some issues, they're not always driven to repair that relationship. Sometimes they just quietly move on. It's no big deal.

When it comes to relationships, men are independent. He operates like the Lone Ranger, not needing anyone to show him how relationships work. (Ok, the Lone Ranger had his friend Tonto and his horse Silver, but that's different.) For most of his life, that approach has served him pretty well. But when he comes into a relationship with a woman he deeply cares about, he can't treat it the same way. He desperately wants to make the relationship work but he feels like he's in a rowboat with no oars in the middle of the ocean.

So, as a woman, what can you do? Later we'll talk about some of the options for helping your man understand you in a way that works for him. For now, it's just helpful to realize what's going on in his head when it comes to relationships, and why they're so tough for him.

He's hardwired for self-sufficiency and needs to feel competent in his abilities. That wiring has been reinforced by his lifelong exposure to culture, media, and other men who say that real men need to just figure it out. His motives are great, but his tool kit is sparse.

From Boys to Men

There's another characteristic of men that's hardwired into his brain: the drive to make a difference, have a purpose, and do something that matters. This is huge. That's why it's so tough for a man when he loses his job; a lot of his identity comes from the contribution he makes at work. When that disappears, his self-confidence often suffers. He doubts himself when he's not able to make that contribution, and that doubt leaks into every area of his life.

A woman might tell her boyfriend, "I don't care if you make a lot of money. I love you for who you are." That's great, and he loves hearing it. But *he* cares about it, even if she doesn't. To him, he gets paid for adding value. The more he makes, the more value he feels he's adding. So he sees the money as a sign that he's making a difference.

He might be worth millions but still want more. It's not the money; it's what the money represents. If he makes more, it means he's contributing more. He's fulfilling his purpose. He's fulfilling one of the greatest needs a man has: making a difference.

Rick Warren's book *The Purpose Driven Life* wasn't expected to hit the bestseller list.[2] But as soon as it was published, it spread like wildfire. The last figures I saw indicated it had sold over thirty million copies and was the second most translated book in history (next to the Bible). In a market that tends to be dominated by female readers, the book found an audience with men as well. I'm guessing it was the title that attracted their attention. Deep inside, men want to have a purpose; it's the driving factor in their life. No wonder so many men picked it up!

For a man, self-esteem is closely tied in to that sense of purpose. It follows that "purpose" becomes part of a man's script from his earliest days.

Insisting on Independence

Put a boy on a playground, and he's trying to find ways to stand out in the crowd through competition and comparison. As he develops his life skills, he's anxious to try them out and see if he can be independent.

Girls might mature earlier than boys, both physically and emotionally. However, boys are usually more anxious to throw off the shackles that tie them down and test their wings. They fight with their parents about restrictions, chafe at regulations at school, and push the limits with the law.

They want to be independent. They want to be adults. Why? It's that inner drive to do something that matters, even if their motives aren't obvious. As long as they're still "a kid," they're restricted from making that contribution.

When boys graduate from high school, they feel free. But they haven't grown up yet. It's common for a bunch of guys to go on a "road trip," where they hop in a car and drive with no destination. It's symbolic of their newfound freedom. After a week or so, they run out of gas, money, or both—and have to call their parents for help.

They have the drive to become responsible adults, but they still want the freedom that comes with adolescence. They've been having fun, probably living at home, and see adult responsibilities as boring and restrictive. They want to grow up, but adulthood and a full-time job seem like a pretty beige lifestyle compared to the one they've been living. When they see it that way, it makes sense that they're in no rush to get there.

When my son-in-law, Brian, graduated from college, he stood with us in the parking lot after the ceremony and had a moment of reality. "I don't want to grow up," he said. He was joking, but I'm sure it had a good helping of accuracy attached.

A lot of guys in that position still live at home, working at a job instead of pursuing a career. It prolongs their adolescence and postpones responsibility. But the longer they delay, the harder it gets. Their self-esteem suffers because they're not making a difference. They've learned how to win at video games but not how to win at life.

Iron Sharpens Iron

Men are influenced by other men. Since they don't ask for help, they observe others to learn how life works. If they're postponing adulthood, it's probable they're watching other guys do the same thing. If they choose to grow up and be responsible, they're probably copying the patterns of other men they respect.

Someone said that we become like the five people we hang out with the most. That's especially true for men. They're crafting their adult life by watching others craft theirs, and they do it by spending time with them.

It's important that a woman recognizes the value that comes from her man's male relationships. Those relationships are going to look totally different from hers, but they meet some of his basic needs that she can't meet. He might adore her, but she can't meet all his needs.

What happens when men get together? What do those relationships look like?

Men tend to be loyal to their friends.

A woman might wonder why he stays connected with an old high school buddy who seems like a total jerk. It usually comes from his sense of loyalty. They might not have much in common, but they've done life together at some point, so they keep some connection.

I have high school friends I haven't seen for decades, but we still connect occasionally on Facebook. I know they're totally different from who they were back then, and so am I. In many cases, we've taken paths that have drawn us apart, not together. But we shared a season together, and it was good.

Men are pretty straightforward in their conversations.

Most men say what they're thinking and aren't afraid to disagree with each other. He's not that worried about how the other guy might feel or respond, because he knows they'll both move past it when they're done talking it out. If they can't get past it, they simply find excuses to not stay connected.

Sure, there's the introvert issue. A lot of men aren't comfortable with confrontation, so they don't say what they're thinking. That doesn't mean they don't have an opinion. It simply means they're choosy about whom they argue with. If it's a relationship that's important to them, they'll find a way to express what they're thinking.

Other times, avoiding confrontation means that he feels the relationship isn't worth the energy to challenge it. He picks his battles, investing in the ones that mean the most to him.

Men don't spend a lot of time talking about the women in their lives.

When men do talk about their women, it's pretty cursory. They don't do a play-by-play recap of a conversation they've had at home. A good man doesn't want to put his woman in a bad light and have his friends think less of her, so he'll protect her reputation. He might make a comment about being frustrated over something, but he won't go into detail. He's not looking for answers or advice, just a little support. When a friend says, "Yeah, I hear you. Sometimes it's tough to know how to respond," he knows he's not alone.

A woman might talk with a trusted female friend about a tough conversation she had with her guy because it helps her sort out what she's feeling. When men are in the same situation, they'll talk about it for thirty seconds and then switch the topic to motor oil.

Men don't usually talk much about their feelings with other men.

Men don't even spend a lot of time thinking about their *own* feelings, much less someone else's. Women say, "What

193

do you *feel* about that?" Men say, "What do you *think* about that?"

Awhile back, I had lunch with a friend who is a pastor of a large congregation, and he told me about a challenging situation he was sorting through with his board. I said, "So, how did that make you feel?" He looked at me blankly and said, "Feel? I don't know. What do you think I am . . . a woman?"

That doesn't mean men don't have feelings. They just might not be aware of what their feelings are, so they resort to their auxiliary backup feelings. If they feel scared or sad or worried, they express it through a male-appropriate backup feeling like anger. In either case, they're not driven to figure them out, and they definitely won't be discussing them with other men.

Men look to other men as a safe place with no expectations.

When life gets hard, men gravitate to other men so they can face it together. They don't have to explain what they're thinking or feeling if they don't want to, and there's no judgment. Hanging out at a ball game with friends and talking about nothing important is great therapy for a man when life gets tough. He's not escaping; he's just recharging so he can reenter the battle of life.

I read once that when women are in a relationship, they tend to face each other (figuratively and literally). When men are in a relationship, they tend to stand side-by-side and face in one direction. From my own experience, I've found that to be pretty accurate. My friends don't try to solve my problems for me. They're willing to walk with me on that journey, and I don't have to explain myself.

Explaining and figuring things out is a lot of work for a guy, so he'll save his energy to do that with the one person who matters most to him—his woman.

Men face challenges together.

Even though men are independent, their loyalty allows them to work well as a team with other guys when they're facing challenges. That's why a sales force builds camaraderie when they're striving for an important goal, or a team works well together on a sports field. It's why soldiers build such a strong commitment to each other when they're in battle.

When men are committed to a goal they consider to be worthwhile, they'll do whatever is necessary to help each other succeed.

In business, people have often found great value in "mastermind groups." It's a small group of people who are committed to growth and success in a specific area, and they know they can reach higher levels of success together than alone. So they meet regularly for new ideas, motivation, and accountability. They challenge each other and provoke each other to dream big and reach levels of success they didn't know were possible.

There's real value in a small group of guys getting together to support each other in their relationships with their women. They know it's not easy to be effective in male/female relationships, but they're committed to making it work. Men need the input of other men to build their skills in relating to women. In fact, a healthy man probably has three types of men in his life:

- Someone older and wiser—a mentor who is a little further ahead on the journey
- Someone younger and less experienced he can mentor who is a little further behind on the journey
- Someone at a peer level he can share the journey with

If your man doesn't have these relationships, he might be missing out on a valuable resource. You could encourage him with casual suggestions like these:

"Have you ever thought of grabbing coffee with (older, wiser man that he respects)?"

"You seem to connect well with (younger, less experienced man), especially since he's on the same path you've been on. Have you ever thought of spending a little time with him, just to be a sounding board for him?"

"Who's your best guy friend who motivates you to grow?"

Driven to Grow

I've had countless conversations over the years with men in their early thirties who are struggling with "growing up." They've been lured by the media and friends into extending their adolescence as long as possible.

At that age, their inner drive to be a responsible adult begins to get stronger and stronger, and they become more and more dissatisfied with those old patterns. The longer they postpone it, the more their self-esteem is damaged because they're not making the difference they were designed to make.

Men are hardwired for independence and competence. It doesn't mean he wants to live his life separately from his woman. It means he can connect with her in a healthy way if he has a strong sense of wholeness. When he feels like he's competent, he's able to be the man his woman needs.

I recently spoke with a thirty-two-year-old who was enjoying his perpetual adolescence—but finally settled down, got serious about his career, and married the woman of his dreams. It changed everything for him. When I asked him what made such a difference, he summarized it well: "I just finally decided it was time to grow up."

13

Turning Two into a Team

I once heard a man say, "Yes, I definitely wear the pants in the family. My wife picked them out, but I definitely wear them."

It's humorous, but it's a good example of how two very different people can work together to get better results. In general, men tend to be better at certain things and women tend to be better at others. When they work together and bring their strengths into the equation, the outcome is better than either of them can produce alone.

Men and women need to be viewed as equal in terms of value, uniqueness, and contribution. That doesn't mean they're exactly the same in every way. If they were, there would be no conflict in relationships but also no potential for growth.

Society and the media have given us pretty shabby portrayals of men and women. When communication doesn't work well between them, most of the public sentiment is that it's the man's fault. He's the one who needs to become more sensitive and listen more and communicate better and express his feelings.

The message a man hears repeatedly is, "You're not good at loving your woman, and you need to change."

As I talked to a number of men when I began writing this book, I consistently heard frustration around that. One man said, "I get that women are more sensitive than us and communicate better. But who said that the woman's view was the right one?"

Another pointed out the things that men tend to do better than most women, such as having more physical strength and driving toward solutions. He said, "How come nobody is telling women they need to step it up and become stronger, talk less, and get to solutions quicker?"

That's an interesting point. Assuming that men and women need to change is like telling a dog and a cat they need to become more like each other if they're going to get along. Nobody questions the craziness of that, since dogs naturally do dog stuff and cats naturally do cat stuff. No one expects a cat to grab a leash and excitedly bug his owner to go for a walk.

The key is in knowing the differences, accepting and respecting them, and working with that reality.

Relationships where differences are mostly *criticized* end up needing repair.

Relationships where differences are *tolerated* end up needing maintenance.

Relationships where differences are consistently *celebrated* thrive and grow.

Cooking Class

Men and women have certain *general* characteristics that are different from each other's. Each individual also has *specific* unique characteristics they bring into the relationship. When you put two people together, you get a much greater mix of characteristics than either person possesses separately. Blending those characteristics creates an unlimited set of outcomes.

It's kind of like cooking in your kitchen. If you only have a few ingredients in your cupboard, it's possible to cook—but your options are limited. If you double the number of ingredients you have on hand, you have a huge potential in the number of dishes you can prepare. You won't use every ingredient every time you cook, but having them available expands the possibilities.

Saying a woman's characteristics are better than a man's is like saying that sugar is better than salt. Sugar brings a certain sweetness to a recipe, and most people love the taste. But if we leave out the salt, the sweetness becomes bland and tasteless. Salt is essential for most recipes to bring out the richness of every other flavor.

Of course, we can overdo it. Too much salt ruins the entire meal. Beginning cooks don't have the experience to know how much to use, so they follow proven recipes that tell them exactly how much of each ingredient to use for the best results. Over time, the cook becomes more experienced and feels the freedom to come up with their own variations. Trial and error often produces results that aren't the best, but they keep trying until they perfect their recipes.

Chefs still have to start with the right ingredients. They have to have sugar. They have to have salt. And they have to know the right amounts to use in a particular recipe.

That's exactly what happens in relationships. It's the differences between men and women that produce the greatest results when used with care in the right combinations. Early in a relationship, men and women are attracted by those differences. If a couple only focuses on wanting the other person to change, they won't be able to create anything new. They'll both stick with the same old recipes they've always known. If they work together to explore and appreciate those differences, a whole world of possibilities opens up for them.

We need to be careful of accepting the media's and society's condemnation of men's inability to love their women properly. If we do, we rob a relationship of the most foundational ingredients that make it thrive—*differences*.

Seeking Synergy

For Mother's Day this year, our grandkids made an arrangement of succulents in a pot for my wife. It was the perfect gift, because they each picked one succulent to contribute and told her why they picked it.

Eleven-year-old Averie picked a green one with a unique pattern. She thought it was special because it would grow fast, producing tiny white blossoms as it grew. She knew Grandma loved flowers.

Eight-year-old Elena chose one with a dark green body and a bright orange and red section at the top. She thought it looked tropical, and she knew that Grandma loved the beach.

Five-year-old Marco picked a bushy, fuzzy green one because he thought it looked like a tarantula.

It's the perfect gift because it exactly expresses their personalities. The girls were into the uniqueness and color, thinking of what Grandma would appreciate. The boy picked one that reminded him of a bug.

So which one is best? Without hesitation, it's the complete arrangement that brings her the most joy. The individuality isn't lost, but the combination is a constant reminder of how those little personalities bring so much richness into our lives when they're together.

It's called *synergy*. Synergy is different things coming together and forming something totally new without losing individuality.

When I think of synergy, two metaphors come to mind: a fruit salad and an orchestra. In a fruit salad, you combine strawberries, peaches, bananas, or other fruits. When they're mixed together, there's a brand-new taste that exists from that combination, yet you can still taste the individual fruits at the same time. In an orchestra, different instruments combine to create a sound that can fill a concert hall, but you still hear the individual instruments.

Once when our kids were little, we took them to a John Williams concert at the Hollywood Bowl. The music was themes they might recognize, including movie and cartoon favorites. They were probably a little too young because they began to lose interest after a while.

A friend handed them a pair of binoculars so they could see the orchestra members close-up. They came up with a game where they tried to see each individual type of instrument playing at the same time they heard it. So when the unique sound of a bassoon or oboe or French horn played, they scanned the orchestra to see who was playing it. By the end of the evening they managed to connect all of the instrument sounds to their players. The combined sound of the orchestra was amazing, but the individual sounds were still there.

That's synergy. It's the differences in a relationship that produce an outcome greater than either person brings by themselves, but they don't lose their uniqueness. When a couple fights over their differences, they lose the potential for producing something great. When they value and celebrate those differences, the results are unlimited.

What If *He's* the Problem?

When Diane and I were first married, I paid the bills and handled the budget. We weren't making much, and money was always tight. She would come to me and ask something like, "Do we have enough money to buy a new throw rug to put in front of the couch?"

Here's where things got interesting. I deeply wanted her to be happy. I also wanted her to see me as a good husband and successful provider. If I said, "No, we don't have the money," she might be disappointed. It would reflect on my effectiveness as well. So I would say, "Sure. Go ahead," whether we had the money or not.

I didn't realize the damage this was causing. With my limited tools and experience at this relationship thing, I wouldn't talk to her about where we were with our finances. My mind automatically went into a solution mode: *I can't say no to the rug. I just need to figure out how to bring more money in.*

It was up to me to fix the problem, not talk with her about it. That would be like asking for help—which is something men don't like to do.

At the same time, it was hard for Diane to ask about our finances because I would become defensive every time she did. To her, it felt like I was shutting her out and being secretive about our money. Deep inside, I felt like I was doing a bad job. My self-esteem was shaky because I couldn't solve the problem. It felt like it was my fault we didn't have enough money, so I couldn't let her know what was really happening.

She wanted to trust me, but she was smart enough to sense that things weren't right. Neither of us knew what to do. I thought she was nagging, and she thought I was irresponsible. We weren't facing the problem together; we were seeing each other as the problem. That created an unspoken wedge between us because we were living on assumptions.

In an immature way, I was hiding those things from her because I cared about her happiness so much and desperately loved her. I wanted the best for her and didn't know how to make it happen. So I avoided the topic. I thought that if we could avoid talking about it, at least nobody would be upset.

You could probably call it pride, but it was more than that. It was a typical male response coming from great motives. Neither of us were talking about the problem or looking together for a solution. We were posturing to see who was right and who was wrong.

A Win-Win Solution

It wasn't until we hit a crisis point that we began to deal with our communication patterns. The financial issue had become the elephant in the room, and we were frustrated with each other because of our differences.

When the outcomes became too obvious to ignore, it forced us to have a tough conversation. It was uncomfortable, because we didn't want to accuse each other (or admit that we were at fault). But once we started talking about how we could work on the problem *together*, we became a team.

One of our biggest realizations was that I was right-brained and creative while she was left-brained and organized. Anytime you put a creative mind in charge of finances, it's a recipe for disaster. Yes, I was solution-driven, but would scramble immediately to any creative solution that might work. She was logical and methodical and wanted to find an outcome that would be a permanent solution to the issue. Her approach tended to be inflexible while mine was like a flock of birds that never landed.

We realized it would be best for her to handle the mechanics of the budget. It would get done, bills would be paid on time, and we would know how much money we had all the time. At the same time, we agreed to talk frequently about our finances to make sure we were on the same page. That allowed me to still feel effective because I was participating in a solution that worked.

It also made me feel like a winner as a husband because we were working together in a way that satisfied both of us. When money got tight, I didn't have to feel like a failure anymore, and she didn't have to deal with my immaturity. We just faced it together and talked about it.

That was years ago, and we're doing pretty well. Those old patterns keep trying to creep in, and we have to remind each other that it's us against the problems, not against each other.

We're a team and we need to keep it that way. When we do, everything is better.

The Power of Kudos

I've heard women say, "Why do I have to pull out the pom-poms and cheer every time he does the slightest little thing? Can't he just accept the fact that I appreciate his efforts?"

Simply stated, no. A man wants to make a difference and be effective and win, and the main place he wants that to happen is with you. He wants to be your hero, whether he says that or not. He's not on an ego trip. He's just a taller version of the little boy on the playground saying, "Look at me!"

Sometimes I'll be working on a project in the garage and hit a situation I can't figure out. I'm stumped and need to take some time to let the problem run around in my mind for a few hours. Eventually it comes together and I find a solution—and it feels awesome. I fought the problem and found a creative solution. I conquered it. I won.

Guess what my next action is? I go in the house and tell Diane what I did. Usually, I'll bring her outside to show her, even though she might not know what she's looking at. Why? I want the pom-poms. Nothing in the world feels better than her gushing over my ability to figure something out. Don't ask me why, because I don't know. It's just the way my brain works. I realize it's not natural for her and she's doing it because she knows how much it means to me. But that makes it even better; she's doing it intentionally, not naturally.

Women want their men to say, "I love you." Men want to express their love but they're not often good with words. It might seem simple enough to say but it's not. Most men express their love with actions more than words. But when a man realizes the importance those words hold for his woman, he'll find a way to say them—even if it's uncomfortable.

In the same way, it's not natural for a woman to bring out the pom-poms and celebrate a man's accomplishments. But it means as much to a man as his tender words do to a woman. Recognition and appreciation are part of the fuel that keeps a man motivated, and the wise woman will provide it for him. It's more than thanking him for what he does (though that's important). It's affirming his abilities in words that meet his needs: "That's awesome. How did you figure that out?"

At the same time, *express* your gratefulness for those little things he does. Don't let them slide by unnoticed. Respond with short, sincere comments such as, "That was nice—thanks," or "Just so you know, I didn't miss the fact that you put the toilet seat down last night, because I didn't fall in. Thanks." If he holds the door open for you, make him feel like a winner by saying, "Wow—that feels great. I don't have many friends whose man opens the door for them."

Or just respond in a female way to his male approach. If he happens to hand you the television remote, pause, look him in the eye, and say, "Thanks. I love you too."

You might be thinking, *Ok, I understand. But what about me? What if I'm doing all this stuff for him but he's not doing any of it for me?*

That's a legitimate question, but it's outside the scope of this book. As we said in the beginning, this is just a book for women about how to understand men. When women understand those differences, they can choose how to respond based on what they discover. Trying to change others is usually futile. But the one person we can always change is ourselves—our attitudes and actions.

It's like dancing with another person. If we change what we do in our dance, the other person is placed in the position of deciding how they're going to dance with us. We decide how we dance. They decide how to respond.

Learn to be grateful for your differences rather than fighting them. That's the best place to start for building synergy and creating a world-class relationship.

14

Relationship Red Flags

I knew what it was right away.

As I approached the steps to go up onto our wooden deck in the backyard, I glanced down. Just in front of the first step, I saw tiny, brown granules on the concrete. I tried to convince myself it was just dirt that had blown up against the step, but I knew from experience what it was: *frass*.

Frass is a fancy word for "termite droppings." I've seen it over the years and knew what it meant. Termites can eat through an entire piece of wood, leaving only a skeletal structure on the inside without touching the outside. That's why termites are so damaging. You don't know any damage is being done because everything looks fine on the outside. But what looks like an intact piece of wood has become a hollow shell. You only realize the problem when your foot goes through the board. Or your house falls down.

But long before that, the frass appears. It's a hint that there's a problem.

I saw the frass, and my mind started running. I immediately started thinking of the cost of calling an exterminator. Then I added the cost of replacing the damaged wood. Then I pictured the hassle of moving out while the house was being tented. I didn't know how much damage had already been done, but I knew there was a problem.

I'm a guy, and I needed a solution. So I grabbed a broom and swept it away.

Problem solved.

Over the next few months, the frass kept reappearing, and I kept sweeping it away. I never mentioned it to my wife, because that would mean I would have to admit (to her and myself) that there was a problem. As long as there was no frass, there was no problem.

Finally, I realized that the frass was appearing more frequently. So we ended up talking about it and decided what to do. I removed the board, treated the steps, and replaced the damaged wood. I had caught it early enough that it wasn't that difficult to fix. We eventually had a professional come and inspect the house because we realized the danger of ignoring termite prevention. There were a few more places that needed treatment, and he took care of them.

The outcome? We don't worry about termites right now because we took care of the problem.

But I'm always on the lookout for frass.

Relationship Frass

When you buy a new house, you do an initial inspection. If you see frass, you give serious thought to the condition of the house. If there's no frass, you assume it's ok and you move in. You're excited about what it will be like living in your new place. Frass is the last thing on your mind, and you start decorating.

That's true in relationships as well. When you first start connecting with a man, you're "inspecting" him. He's interesting and he looks good. You can see yourself being in a relationship with him. You look for frass, deciding if he's a solid investment or not. If you don't see it, you move forward with excitement and assume everything is ok.

Sometime later, you notice the little frass pellets. You catch a look you haven't seen before, or hear an attitude in his voice, or sense an unfamiliar frustration. It's barely on your consciousness and it feels uncomfortable. You don't want to address it because you don't want to question this exciting new relationship. So you sweep it away.

Soon it happens again. Then it becomes more frequent but you hope it's not a real problem. After a while you see a pattern and you can't ignore it any longer.

When you bring it up he becomes defensive and upset. Over time it becomes an "untouchable" area. Your relationship suffers and your communication is unhealthy. It feels like it's never going to change, and you've lost the opportunity to have the healthy relationship we've been discussing in previous chapters.

Is it too late? Is there hope?

Simply stated, it's never too late as long as both parties are still breathing. People can change, and often do when least expected (and for the quirkiest reasons). There is *always* hope.

There are *never* guarantees.

Early Detection

We're assuming here that the relationship hasn't become toxic. When there are serious issues, a book like this will guide you toward understanding what those issues are but it won't solve them. For that, you may need professional help. When relationships are damaged, there's not a quick fix.

If I scratch my finger, I grab a bandage and some antiseptic to start the healing. But if a cancerous tumor appears, I'll need the skills of an experienced medical professional.

The severity of the problem determines the appropriate treatment. Some of the symptoms to watch for might include some of the following:

- Your man tends to be generally negative during conversations.
- He tries to manipulate you by saying things like, "If you really cared about me, you would stay home tonight instead of going to that yoga class."
- He uses absolutes: "You never . . ." or "You always . . ."
- He uses humor to deflect conflict.
- He changes the subject whenever things get uncomfortable.
- He minimizes your opinion: "Oh, just let it go. You're being unreasonable."
- He never has an opinion, and just gives in to whatever you want to keep the peace.

Most people respond in one or more of these ways from time to time. If your man shows one of these symptoms occasionally, it doesn't mean there's a major problem. The two things to look for are *number* and *frequency.* The more of these symptoms you see and the more frequently they appear, the greater the need to address the situation.

The question is, "How do I deal with those red flags in my relationship?"

Fear of Frass

Some women are afraid to bring up tough issues with their man, especially early in a relationship. They're afraid of losing him, so they pretend everything is ok. That is building the relationship on a base of dishonesty, keeping it from going deep because you're not letting him inside. Over time you begin to resent him because the issue isn't going away. He senses this and pulls away even further. It's not fair to him because you haven't said anything.

As a woman gets frustrated over these unresolved issues, and she doesn't know what to do, she might confront him or lash out, telling him in so many words that he needs to get his act together. It's the only thing she knows that will get some type of reaction from him. *If I don't somehow keep after him, he'll never change.*

Whether she says it aloud or thinks it to herself, that last sentence is the heart of the problem. A woman's most common response to relationship difficulties is to feel like her life will never improve until her man changes. Unfortunately, that attitude can be a recipe for disaster. It makes two assumptions:

1. You can change another person.
2. The other person is the problem.

We talked about this a bit earlier in this book, but let's revisit both of those assumptions individually.

Assumption #1—You can change another person.

My book *People Can't Drive You Crazy If You Don't Give Them the Keys* focuses on the futility of basing our happiness on another person's choices.[1] Anytime our personal sense of wholeness comes from what another person does, it lets us see ourselves as a victim. We're no longer taking responsibility for our life; we've given it to another person. As Eleanor Roosevelt purportedly said, "No one can make you feel inferior without your consent."[2]

A healthy relationship is made of two healthy people, not two half-healthy people hoping to become whole. I can't force another person to change, but I can influence them. How? By changing the one person I *do* have control over: myself. When I grow and change, the other person is living with a different person. When that happens, it's natural for them to respond differently to that "new" person.

There are some things a man can change and some things he can't. If he's practicing bad behavior, that's something he can work on and make better choices. He needs to make those changes. But if his response is because of how he's wired as a man, trying to change him can only lead to frustration.

Assumption #2—The other person is the problem.

"Well, isn't it obvious?" you might ask. "Everything was fine with me, but now he comes into the picture and messes it all up."

Now, let's stand back and look at that statement objectively. Someone on the outside would say, "That sounds a little arrogant." It implies that the woman's way of doing things is correct and the man needs to change. It leaves out the fact that she might need to adapt to his way of doing things too, and implies that the only solution is for him to become more like a woman—and the chance of that happening is nonexistent.

Bringing two people together into a relationship doesn't work if it reduces one person or the other. A relationship works when both people come together with all their uniqueness and differences and become a team. On that team, they become something stronger together than either of them are separately. They experience synergy.

How to Change a Man

What's the best way to approach a man when he's gone beyond the frass stage and you're sensing that he's become hollow inside? There's a solution that has a better chance of working, even though it's not guaranteed. It's much better than confronting and attacking him, which is almost always guaranteed to *not* work.

It happens when you accept his maleness and embrace it rather than trying to change it.

That's probably not the solution you were looking for. It probably feels like you're giving up any hope of him changing and you're going to have to live with his stuff forever.

Remember, we're not talking about bad behavior. If he always leaves a mess in the kitchen right after you've cleaned it, he's disrespecting you. That's bad behavior, and it's something he can change (and needs to). We're talking about those characteristics that are there because he's a man.

We've seen that a man has a hardwired need to feel effective and make a difference. For a good man, the place he most wants to see that happen is in his relationship with you.

When you notice things that irritate you, it's easy to make assumptions about his motives. You feel like his feelings toward you are negative and he's on a mission to make your life miserable. That's a dangerous assumption, because he could very well be trying to love you well—but it's not working the way he intended. He tries, but he sees you focusing on what you're not getting rather than what his intent is. That's frustrating for him because he doesn't know how to solve the problem (and he's all about solving problems).

Let's say you've spent the last hour cleaning and polishing the wood floor in the kitchen. The next time you walk through, you see his dusty footprints. Your first reaction is frustration or anger: *I just worked hard on that floor, and he comes in and messes it up. Doesn't he care that I spent so much time making it look nice?*

Yes, he cares—or he would if he had noticed. He doesn't notice dirt. *He also doesn't see clean.* If he didn't see you working on the floor, he probably didn't notice the floor looking any different. Consider how this might look from his perspective.

Maybe, at the same time, he was outside working on a flowerbed you asked him to build. He was doing it because he wanted to make you happy. He was focused on the project and excited to show you. He's that little boy again saying, "Look at what I did!" The clean floor was not even on his radar.

Suddenly he's in trouble. He wasn't being malicious or intentional about messing up your floor. He was just being a man and didn't notice the floor because his focus was some-where else. It doesn't mean you can't talk about it with him. But your reaction needs to come from understanding how he thinks and how excited he is rather than from an assumption about his motives.

It's easier to clean the dirt off the floor than to repair his broken spirit. Ignore the floor this time, and go share his excitement over the flowerbed. Let him know how much you appreciate it and what a good job he did. When you both go back into the house, you could kindly say, "Whoops! I think we're bringing some dirt in from outside. Would you mind wiping your feet before you come in? Thanks!"

If you're not accepting his natural characteristics, it's easy to focus on how they're impacting you. You're thinking about how bad you feel about what he's doing. You put up barriers to protect yourself, such as believing that your perception of his motives is accurate. You don't let him in because you don't want to get hurt.

In relationships where people irritate each other constantly, the root cause is often wishing the other person would change instead of accepting the reality of who they are.

When people finally learn to accept each other as they are wired, everybody gets to relax. When you both feel accepted for who you are as individuals, you both feel safe. You get to be yourself in the relationship. That's when real growth can take place.

It's also interesting that the things we're most irritated by in relationships are often the very things that attracted us to each other in the first place. You fell in love with his strong personality, but now it feels overbearing. You loved his quiet confidence, but now he doesn't talk.

You think, *What happened? Why did he change?* He didn't. You now simply see both sides of that characteristic.

Escaping the Prison Camp

Viktor Frankl, the Austrian psychologist who wrote *Man's Search for Meaning* after his time in a Nazi concentration camp, said, "When we are no longer able to change a situation, we are challenged to change ourselves."[3] He watched people in the worst circumstances give up and die when they focused on the circumstances they had no control of while others survived in the same situation by focusing on their responses to those circumstances.

You might feel like you're imprisoned and there's no hope of anything changing. You're trapped, and it's all his fault. You're sure he'll never change and you fantasize about escape. What's the solution?

It goes back to the Serenity Prayer, penned by Reinhold Niebuhr:

> God, grant me the serenity to accept the things I
>   cannot change,
> The courage to change the things I can,
> And the wisdom to know the difference.[4]

Anytime we try to change another person, we're operating from the belief that they're wrong and need to change. It's their problem. They're the problem. We're right, so nothing will change unless they change. But look at the implications of those three lines of the prayer:

Things I cannot change—the characteristics of his manhood and the unique traits that make up his personality and temperament.

Things I can [change]—the behaviors he has picked up over his lifetime that influence the relationship.

Wisdom to know the difference—we're careful not to mix up the two.

If you focus only on the things you can't change, you'll always be a victim. Accepting their reality is the foundation for freedom.

The Bottom Line

The time to deal with frass is when it first appears. It's a symptom of a potential problem that can damage a relationship if it's not dealt with early.

How do you deal with relationship frass? By communicating about it and accepting each other and your uniqueness. You're dealing with the frass as a team, not ignoring it in isolation.

When both people feel that they are accepted for who they are, it gives them the freedom to dream of a frass-free life.

15

Strategies for
Happy Endings

Can a storybook relationship have a happy ending?

I think I was in seventh grade when I first read a story that didn't. Until then, stories I read always had happy endings. There might be risk and conflict, but everything worked out in the end.

My teacher assigned "To Build a Fire," a 1908 story written by Jack London.[1] We read it in class. It's the story of a man in the Yukon who gets caught in sub-zero conditions and begins to freeze to death. He tries to build a fire, but can't hold the matches because his hands are frozen.

Finally, he gets the fire started (and I can see the happy ending in sight). But the snow on a branch overhead drops onto the fire and puts it out. The man tries everything he can, but things only get worse and worse. Eventually, he lies down and falls asleep—permanently. His dog picks up the "scent of death" and heads back to camp.

I remember sitting at my school desk, trying to comprehend what had just happened. It took days for me to shake off the impact. For the first time, I realized that life didn't guarantee happy endings.

When we're kids, we expect happy endings. As adults, we still want them, though we've learned that happy endings are pretty unpredictable. We know that there are no guarantees, but that doesn't stop us from hoping and trying for them.

Investing in a Storybook Ending

Most relationships start with a storybook ending in mind. Couples think, *It's too bad for everyone else. Nobody has ever had what we have together.* They really believe they have something special (and they do), and that it will lead to a happy ending.

Over time, those relationships get tough. They're made up of real people with real issues, and that causes friction. Some couples split apart when that friction occurs because they've given up on the ending. It's too hard and hopeless. They quit working on the relationship, until it finally shrivels and fades away.

Other couples grow in those tough times. They see those challenges as stepping-stones to make them stronger, and they face them together. It takes a huge effort, but they desperately want the storybook ending. They've decided that the ending is worth risking everything for, even though it's not a guarantee.

They realize that the more energy they put into that relationship, the greater the payoff potential at the other end.

It's kind of like investing. We observe people like Warren Buffett, who is one of the most respected investors on the planet. People see that he's a multibillionaire (happy ending), so they buy the same stocks he buys and wonder why they can't even afford a vanilla latte with their returns. What they overlook is how long he's been investing, making small, intentional choices over a lifetime.

People want to make a killing in the stock market. They start with high hopes but get nervous when the market fluctuates. Their dream becomes a nightmare. Warren Buffett takes advantage of tough markets, using commonsense strategies no matter what the economy does. He sticks with basic, proven principles of investing and wealth management.

We can do that with our relationships too. We don't know what's ahead in our journey. But we can apply investing principles to those relationships to get the highest possible return on our investment.

If we want a storybook ending, we need to be intentional about making it happen. Knowing that it's not guaranteed, we can commit to the work it takes over time to aim for the results we desire. Those consistent patterns lead to predictable results, both in investing and in relationships.

Investments of the Heart

Here are a few principles about financial investing that apply when you're investing in a relationship with a man.

Invest in what you know.

In the financial world, too many people make investment decisions based on a "hot tip" they heard in the media and then wonder why they don't make a boatload of cash right away. The genuine experts suggest that we should never invest in anything we don't fully understand.

If you're going to give your heart to a man, it shouldn't be a casual commitment. He's worth studying for a lifetime. The more you know about him, the more you'll feel comfortable investing. If you become an expert in that particular man, you'll have the best chance possible for a successful relationship with him.

Don't get spooked when the market dives.

When a stock goes up, people get excited and buy it. When a stock goes down, they panic and get rid of it. Healthy investing does the opposite, buying when the market is low and building that investment until the market is high to maximize their return.

Life has its ups and downs, and men aren't immune to those changes. When life gets tough and a man gets down, some women jump out of a relationship because it's not going the way they expected. That's often the best time to make an even greater investment, starting a growth process for when the "market" goes up. It takes commitment and courage on your part, but it's the only way to get the highest level of return.

In a marriage relationship, this means keeping the promises you made on your wedding day when you committed to each other "for better or for worse." Tough times don't feel good, but they're the seedbed for growth.

Use the compounding effect.

Little investments made consistently for a long time take advantage of compounding interest. At first, it seems like you're only earning pennies on the dollar. But by reinvesting those pennies, the principal grows—and you make interest on that larger balance. Do it for a long enough time and the account grows exponentially.

You can't pour a bunch of attention into a man once in a while and expect big results. You also can't make regular emotional withdrawals, because it reverses the compounding effect. The best way to grow your investment in a man is to make constant, consistent, tiny everyday deposits that multiply over time. It protects the principal so it can keep growing.

There are no get-rich-quick schemes in relationships. It takes patience and persistence. Your investment will grow, and the dividends can be substantial over time.

Work with a professional.

Uncle Larry might have made a lot of money with his style of investing, but that doesn't mean his is the path you should follow. Investment "experts" in the media give financial advice, but it doesn't matter to them if it works for you or not. An experienced financial planner who cares about you and your success is a valued resource for growing wealth. They're a strategic partner, not just an advice giver. They have the training and experience to see small issues that can be addressed before they become major ones.

I don't try to install air-conditioning, rebuild my car's engine, or do surgery on myself. For important things like that, I hire an expert to do what they're highly trained to do.

Relationships don't grow well in isolation. We're too close to the important issues and dynamics to figure it all out. That's why we do life with other people, so we share the journey.

And when it looks like the road ahead is impossible to pass, we call in an expert.

I grew up in Arizona. As teenagers, we tried to get as much sun as possible. We even used tanning oils to magnify the sun's rays. Nobody thought it was a bad thing.

Years later, I now make Lexus payments for my dermatologist. I see him once or twice a year, and he freezes off my precancerous spots before they grow into something serious. I can't even see or feel those spots, but his expertise, training, and experience allow him to find those things and remove them when they first appear. The treatment isn't always comfortable, but he's keeping me from getting skin cancer later.

I'm a huge believer in therapists and professional counselors for relationship issues. It's common for men to feel like a failure if they need to get help. But that perspective implies we should be capable of solving all our own problems. Nice idea, but unrealistic.

Men struggle with this issue frequently because of their desire to be "in control." They wait until the problem has gotten out of control before seeking help. They figure that if they ignore the issue it will take care of itself over time. But it only grows like an emotional cancer that can destroy a relationship if it's not dealt with.

The solution? Talk with your man about the value of getting a relationship "tune-up" while things are going well, instead of waiting for major issues to come up. It's less threatening for him if he doesn't think he's going to get put on the spot and feel attacked. Suggest that, in the same way you both get an annual "physical" exam, maybe you could also have an annual "relationship" exam with a skilled professional.

Schedule an appointment for a tune-up, and let the therapist explore and deal with those tiny spots before they become cancerous. It's a chance to do preventative work before a small issue turns into a giant one.

Creating High Returns

We've been on a journey in this book to understand the way a man thinks and how it's different from the way a woman thinks. Looking through the eyes of a man for understanding is the foundation for a world-class relationship. Once that foundation is in place, you can begin investing in that man for growth.

If you try a few of the things we've suggested in this book, you're implementing your investment strategy. Those small, consistent actions have a great chance of growing into a highly satisfying relationship. There are no quick fixes or easy solutions, just commonsense caring over time.

If I were to handpick a few of the most important strategies we've talked about in this book for investing in your man, here are the simplest ones I've found that lead to the highest lifetime return.

Constantly look through his eyes to see his perspective.

Seeing another person's perspective is never natural, so you have to choose to do it for the rest of your life. The more you accept the genuine differences your man has and adapt to their reality, the freer you'll be to become his true partner. It also frees him to become the kind of man he was designed to be.

Waste time together.

Most men don't get excited about spending time talking about their relationship and analyzing their feelings. They just want to enjoy their woman, and that usually happens when they spend time together just messing around. Meet your man's need for companionship and activity without pushing the relationship issues too much, and he'll probably be much more inclined to discuss them when it's appropriate.

He's simple, and he's mostly interested in enjoying you. Let him do it, and make it a priority.

Make laughter a priority in your relationship.

When life gets complicated, it's natural to hunker down and take everything seriously. Life *is* serious. But allowing "lightness" into the relationship makes it easier for him to be serious. Movies use comic relief to break the tension during stressful moments, and relationships need to do the same.

My wife and I were talking with some friends a couple of years ago about handling the tough stuff in our relationships. They asked how we handled some of those situations, and we described the way we interact. It's usually a combination of serious discussion and playfulness.

The woman said, "Well, I think you guys are just happier than most people." I thought about that for a long time. It's probably true, but not because life is always cheery. I think we've been intentional about enjoying each other, whether circumstances are good or bad. It helps us work together as a team, knowing that facing the problem together makes us both stronger.

Your man connected with you initially because it seemed more enjoyable than being by himself. If the relationship loses that playfulness, it gets heavy and tedious. If you commit to playfulness, he can enjoy you no matter what life brings.

Show him respect whenever you can, in little and big ways.

Respect is a huge need for a man, and it will determine how successful he is in handling life. If he knows you respect him with all his imperfections, it will give him the strength to be the kind of man you want him to be. It's easy to take that need for granted because it's probably not as strong a need for you. Never forget that he needs respect the way a parched person needs water.

Clarify expectations.

Recognize that you're always looking at the same thing through different lenses. Make sure you clarify each other's lenses before making assumptions.

For example, he's heading to a convenience store and says, "Hey, do you want me to bring you anything?" You respond, "Sure—bring me an apple." In your mind, you're picturing a large, crisp, cold, crunchy red apple. Instead, he brings home a small, mushy yellow one because it's all they had. He did what you asked, and in his mind he met your need. But you had a different expectation, and you're disappointed.

Differing expectations is one of the biggest reasons men and women have trouble connecting. Take the time to clarify what your man is thinking (and clarify your own expectations), and you'll save a lot of grief in the future.

Take care of yourself.

Get healthy and keep growing. Don't let your view of yourself be based on how he performs (or doesn't) as a man. He might be growing or responding, or he might be struggling. Don't go down with him. Eat right, get enough sleep, and invest in yourself. You need to be a whole person if you're planning to build a whole relationship.

Be intentional.

The more important something is and the more value it has, the more attention it deserves. A man you're in a relationship with will be the biggest potential investment you'll ever make and has the potential for the biggest possible return. Study him, grow with him, and believe in him. Make intentional effort to help him become the best version of himself possible.

The Potential for Greatness

Investing is always an attempt to balance risk and reward. You can find security and safety in a savings account at the bank, but you'll only make pennies in interest. Low risk, low reward. If you want high reward, you'll have to invest in some things that have high potential, but no guarantees.

A man is like that. When you make an emotional investment in a man, you're hoping for the best. You could play it safe and try to maintain the relationship the way it is, hoping things will turn out ok. That strategy might keep a relationship together, but it won't thrive.

Or you could see your man as a blue-chip investment. He's loaded with potential, and there's the possibility of seeing your investment multiply astronomically. Sure, there's risk—you never know how it will turn out. Maybe his "stock price" is low at the moment. The more you study him and become intentional about building into his life, the greater chance you have of achieving greatness in your relationship.

A lot of people settle for relationship mediocrity because it's the result they get from taking the easy road. But if you accept the challenge and build your "portfolio" around your man, you're setting up your relationship to reach heights you couldn't imagine. As Buzz Lightyear said in the movie *Toy Story*, "To infinity . . . and beyond."[2]

Here are three specific things about your man to keep in mind:

1. His potential for greatness as a man is unlimited.
2. You have more of an impact on him reaching that greatness than anyone else in the world.
3. If he feels your support and respect, he'll usually do anything for you and the relationship. In other words, he'll invest back in the relationship to make it great.

This book is simply a template for how to approach the man in your life. There's no secret formula for success in relationships. You can never predict what a man will do in response to your choices. But if you make those choices based on his interests, priorities, and needs, you've raised the odds for him to respond in a new, positive way.

So really, you're not working on him; you're working on you.

A lot of books say that a woman needs to change to become what her husband expects and wants. That misses the entire point of this book.

The key isn't to become something you're not, giving up part of yourself just to please him. It means becoming all that you can be, keeping your integrity, and fostering your true self.

At the same time, do so with an understanding of what happens in the mind of a man. When you see life from his perspective, you can make the best choices for both of you.

If you start with becoming your own healthiest self, it's tough for him not to respond differently to you. After all, you've become a different person (in a sense). When you change, chances are he'll see you in a new way and respond accordingly.

Take the Plunge

You picked up this book because you were having trouble understanding your man, right? You were hoping for insights and formulas and suggestions that would make your relationship stronger, but you weren't sure what that might look like.

My goal has been to let you peek inside your man's brain. I can't make choices for you and I can't fix relationships that are broken. No book can do that. All I can do is be a tour guide to point out the features you might not know are there and explain some of the pitfalls that seem treacherous. And hopefully, this book has given you a new perspective about your man.

It's up to you where you go from here. Maybe your relationship needs some honest conversation about your differences.

Maybe it needs some clarification of expectations. Maybe it needs an injection of humor, or compassion, or humility. Maybe it needs professional guidance. Maybe it needs time.

The place to start is with understanding. Without knowing how a man thinks, all of your attempts to improve your relationship will be short-lived. If you have that base of understanding, the potential for growth is limitless.

He didn't come with instructions.

Maybe it's time to invite him to write those instructions together.

Acknowledgments

've learned a few things after writing five books.

- They get easier because you learn how to write better from writing more.
- They get harder because you want them to be better. So you study more and think more.
- You do it alone, which means hours and hours spent sitting and thinking and typing. When you talk to someone, you're not writing.
- You never do it alone. There are always people in your life who make you successful. In my case, it tends to be the same people for each book.

I'm spoiled to have had the world's best editor for all of my books (in my humble but absolutely correct opinion). When Vicki Crumpton renovates a manuscript, it transforms from a pimply teenager to a responsible adult. When she's done polishing, it still has the author's voice—but it has matured so it doesn't crack anymore. It's a gift, and I'm continuously grateful for the partnership.

Joel Kneedler is the epitome of what an agent is supposed to be like. He shepherded this project from its inception and has invested personally and professionally in both our relationship and my work. It has been a privilege to work together on my last two books. Unfortunately (for me), a major publisher has recognized that compassion and competence and scooped him up into a more influential role with them. It's well deserved, and I'm proud to see the path he's taken. My loss, but I'm proud of him.

Dr. Dennis Chernekoff has spent his career as a marriage and family therapist, deeply impacting people who struggle through the kinds of issues that come up in this book. He cares about the people he encounters, and his compassion leaks into his everyday relationships. His careful oversight of my thoughts and words keeps me from wandering into the land of crazy ideas. I value his friendship, as well as the time he has invested in this project.

Without my wife, Diane, this book wouldn't exist. All of the ideas in this book have been shaped in the crucible of our relationship over the years. She's talked me through ideas as I was writing, critiqued my words from a woman's perspective, and stayed my best friend. At the end of this process, we still like each other. She makes the journey worth traveling.

My family brings me joy. My friends give me energy. My colleagues challenge my thinking and help me grow. My readers give me the motivation to keep writing. And God gives me perspective and grace, reminding me what matters most.

I always enjoy writing this section, because it reminds me that no one is in this journey alone. For that, I'm reminded to be grateful.

Thanks.

Notes

Chapter 3 Gray Matters

1. Molly Edmonds, "Do Men and Women Have Different Brains?" *How Stuff Works*, accessed December 11, 2015, http://science.howstuffworks.com/life/inside-the-mind/human-brain/men-women-different-brains1.htm.

2. Bjorn Carey, "Men and Women Really Do Think Differently," *Live Science*, January 20, 2005, http://www.livescience.com/health/050120_brain_sex.html.

3. Edmonds, "Do Men and Women Have Different Brains?"

4. Robert Heinlein, "Robert Heinlein Quotes," *World of Quotes*, accessed December 11, 2015, http://www.worldofquotes.com/author/Robert+Heinlein/1/index.html.

Chapter 5 Man on a Mission

1. Kevin Leman, *The Birth Order Book* (Grand Rapids: Revell, 2009).

Chapter 6 Why He Can't See Dirt

1. Mike Bechtle, *People Can't Drive You Crazy If You Don't Give Them the Keys* (Grand Rapids: Revell, 2012).

Chapter 7 Your Knight in Rusting Armor

1. Shaunti Feldhahn, *For Women Only* (Colorado Springs: Multnomah Books, 2013), chap. 2.

2. Ken Blanchard, "75 Years with Ken Blanchard—Looking Back and Looking Ahead," *Ignite!*, May 2014, http://www.kenblanchard.com/Lead ing-Research/Ignite-Newsletter/May-2014.

Chapter 8 Unconditional Like

1. Proverbs 15:1.

Chapter 9 Do Guys Even *Have* Feelings?

1. "All in the Family," *Wikipedia*, accessed December 11, 2015, https://en.wikipedia.org/wiki/All_in_the_Family.

2. Edmonds, "Do Men and Women Have Different Brains?"

3. "10 Things You Chicks Should Really Understand about Us Guys," *Hub Pages*, December 30, 2014, http://hubpages.com/relationships/10 -Things-You-Chicks-Should-Really-Understand-about-Us-Guys.

4. "Six Things Men Wish They Could Tell Women," *eHarmony*, accessed December 11, 2015, http://www.eharmony.com/dating-advice /relationships/six-things-men-wish-they-could-tell-women/#.Vkjirk2FOrU.

5. Dr. Alan Francis, *Everything Men Know about Women* (Riverside, NJ: Andrews McMeel Publishing, 1995).

6. "10 Things You Chicks Should Really Understand about Us Guys."

7. "Six Things Men Wish They Could Tell Women."

8. Robi Ludwig, "Honey, Did You Hear Me? Why Men Don't Listen," *Today Health*, October 27, 2009, http://www.today.com/id/33495762 /ns/today-today_health/t/honey-did-you-hear-me-why-men-dont-listen /#.VkjiNKPTmrU.

9. James Michael Sama, "Actions Speak Louder Than Words: 12 Ways Men Show Their Love," *Huffington Post*, March 13, 2015, http://www.huff ingtonpost.com/james-michael-sama/actions-speak-louder-than-words -12-ways-men-show-their-love_b_6851744.html.

Chapter 11 Conflict without Combat

1. Brian Luke Seaward, *Managing Stress: Principles and Strategies for Health and Well-Being* (Burlington, MA: Jones & Bartlett Learning, 2011), chap. 6.

Chapter 12 The Lone Ranger in Relationships

1. Bruce Feirstein, *Real Men Don't Eat Quiche* (New York: Pocket Books, 1982).

2. Rick Warren, *The Purpose Driven Life* (Grand Rapids: Zondervan, 2002).

Chapter 14 Relationship Red Flags

1. Bechtle, *People Can't Drive You Crazy If You Don't Give Them the Keys.*
2. Eleanor Roosevelt, "Eleanor Roosevelt Quotes," *Brainy Quote,* accessed December 11, 2015, http://www.brainyquote.com/quotes/quotes/e/eleanorroo161321.html.
3. Viktor Frankl, *Man's Search for Meaning* (Boston: Beacon Press, 2000), 112.
4. James Stuart Bell and Jeanette Gardner Littleton, *Living the Serenity Prayer: True Stories of Acceptance, Courage, and Wisdom* (Avon, MA: Adams Media, 2007), 3.

Chapter 15 Strategies for Happy Endings

1. Jack London, *To Build a Fire and Other Stories* (New York: Bantam Classics, 1986).
2. "Buzz Lightyear," *Wikipedia,* accessed December 11, 2015, https://en.wikipedia.org/wiki/Buzz_Lightyear.

Mike Bechtle has a unique blend of corporate and ministry experience—from eighteen years in churches and Christian universities to more than three thousand seminars on productivity, leadership, and communication taught to many of the Fortune 500 companies. He is the author of *People Can't Drive You Crazy If You Don't Give Them the Keys, How to Communicate with Confidence,* and *You Can't Text a Tough Conversation*; his articles have appeared in publications such as *Writer's Digest, Entrepreneur, Discipleship Journal, Moody, Eternity,* and Pastors.com. He has been speaking at corporate events, conventions, and in ministry settings since 1974. After receiving his master's degree at Talbot School of Theology, he received his doctorate in higher and adult education from Arizona State University. Currently a senior training consultant for FranklinCovey Company, Mike lives in Fullerton, California.

For information about speaking engagements, keynotes, and seminars, or to read Mike's current thoughts on his popular blog, visit www.mikebechtle.com.

FOR MORE
COMMUNICATION TOOLS,
PRACTICAL INSIGHT,
AND MOTIVATION, VISIT

MIKEBECHTLE.COM
@MIKEBECHTLE

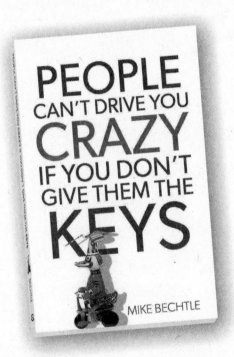

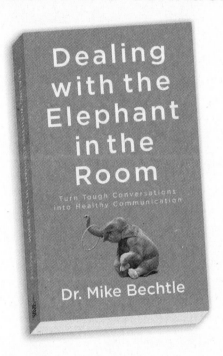

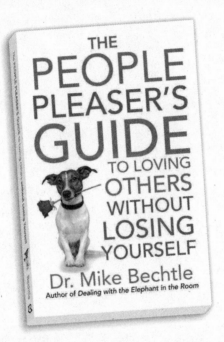

Be the First to Hear about New Books from Revell!

Sign up for announcements about new and upcoming titles at

RevellBooks.com/SignUp

@RevellBooks

Don't miss out on our great reads!

a division of Baker Publishing Group
www.RevellBooks.com